HEALY, REPORTER

- The Early Years -

BY

JOHN HEALY

THE HOUSE OF HEALY

HEALY, REPORTER

ISBN 0 9512639 27

This edition published 1991 by The House of Healy, Achill.

Printed by the Leinster Leader Ltd., Naas, Co Kildare.

John Healy, the author, spent all his working life in journalism. This is the story of his exuberant apprenticeship which moulded the man who was to become *the* journalist of his day. He joined the *Western People*, Ballina, as a cub reporter in 1948 and moved to Dublin in 1950 to join the Irish News Agency. Later he worked with the *Irish Press* Group before joining the *Irish Times* organisation in 1959, to become the youngest editor of a national newspaper, the *Sunday Review* . He went on to edit Ireland's oldest evening paper, the *Evening Mail*.

As a freelance journalist he won the 1967 Television Scriptwriter of the Year Award, published his first book, *No One Shouted Stop*, which has become an important source book on the evolution of modern Ireland as well as being a best-seller. Following its publication Healy was elected "Mayoman of the Year" for "the moral courage and integrity" he had shown in his writings. For close on two decades Healy was the outstanding columnist as Backbencher, first in the *Review*, then in the *Irish Times*, and in one major study to date of the Irish media, Healy is described as "the father of modern political journalism in Ireland".

In 1985 he wrote the best-seller *Nineteen Acres* which portrays life in the basic unit, the family smallholding. A book which can rank with works of Liam O'Flaherty.

Always the environment engaged his mind. In addition to being a director of the Matthew Gallagher R.H.A. Gallery, he was also a member of the National Heritage Council. He founded and edited the magazine *Environment Ireland*. In 1989 he was awarded an Honorary Doctorate by the N.C.E.A. Generally credited with being "one of the few to make sense out of the European maze", in 1990 he was appointed Presidential Spokesperson to represent the Taoiseach at the European Parliament in Strasbourg for the duration of the Irish Presidency.

Healy, Reporter

ONE

You knew from the way Tommy Battle skulked behind the case of type, eyes on the reporter's desk, that he wanted a caption done. Tommy was a compositor in the *Western People* and I was the office cub. Cubs were a good mark for a caption, or headline, for Tommy. I knew now as he circled and watched he was waiting a chance to bone me to write a caption for him. Tommy had been out at the week-end with his little brownie box camera and now he had some picture or other he wanted to send to the Dublin papers.

I had my first six or seven months over me as a trainee reporter and had learned to peck out a two-fingered story on the ancient office typewriter and I knew any minute now, with the foreman at the other end of the works, Battle would dive on me with the request. It would be another of his local weddings or a single column picture of the local sergeant being transferred. Or maybe the local school's first communion contingent. Five minutes would do it - but you made Battle sweat. It was part of the ritual: otherwise he'd haunt you every day. Battle took his chance when he got it. He showed me a print of a young boy with a number of grown men flanking him on either side. Some had pitchforks.

"It's a first communion picture" he explained.

"And where the Jesus are they going with the pitchforks?"

"It's Ernie O'Malley's son - he made his first communion last Sunday an' they were protectin' him."

CHAPTER ONE

I looked at it again. Ernie O'Malley, author and Irish freedom fighter, was a big newsmaker just then. More precisely, his estranged wife was page one news in two continents. An American millionairess, she had fought Ernie O'Malley for the custody of their children after the marriage went on the rocks. She lost the case but subsequently succeeded in snatching the two older children, flying to America with them. And now her third child Cormac, making his first communion, had done so with a bodyguard of local neighbours who feared he too might be snatched by Mrs. Helen Hooker O'Malley.

"I'm sending it to the Sunday Independent - they might use it" said Battle urgently. The urgency was for fear the foreman would see him away from his comping cases.

"Was there anyone else there Tommy?"

"No, why?"

"Ye're not sending it to the *Independent*. Keep it until tonight and I'll write a story for you."

"You're puttin' me off - why can't you write the caption and be done with it?"

"Because we're going to get more for that than thirty bob"

Tommy was puzzled. He wasn't sure of me. After all I was the cub and cubs didn't talk like that.

"You have no correspondence" he said.

'Correspondence' was the great thing for a provincial reporter: you were on your way when you became the local correspondent for the national dailies or weeklies or the Fleet Street, London papers. Generally you had to have achieved senior reporter or news editor status before you inherited the correspondence from more senior men who were moving to Dublin and metropolitan journalism. The editor-proprietor Fredrick V. de Vere had the best of it: he was the area stringer for the Irish Independent Group. It would be two or three years yet that a cub like myself would inherit correspondence. In the meantime stories which I brought in would be 'milked' by my editor who'd put a press pass on them and telegraph them to Dublin on his way home from the office. If you "pulled" him for using your story, he'd nod his head brusquely and say yes he had sent "a few lines" of it to Dublin and he'd look after you when the lineage cheque came at the end of the month. He would split the seven shillings and six-pence with you: it wasn't inconsiderable when you were working for one pound a week and paying two pounds and five shillings for your accommodation.

You had to learn fast in those days in 1948 and I was learning. I had been in the job three weeks when I came across a delightful romantic story involving an American G.I. and an Irish nurse who had met in wartime England. They had parted in a row just before the G.I. shipped out to Europe, but in the four years which followed he could not forget his Kathleen McNulty. He returned to Britain to try and trace her. She had left the hospital and a succession of other hospitals but along the way he had picked up the clue that she was from Mayo in Ireland. Someone else told him that the name McNulty was a strong family name in the Swinford area of Mayo. He came to Mayo in a last, forlorn effort, only to find that there were several nurses of that name who had trained in Britain during the war. But no one could recall a Kathleen McNulty. A local barman directed him to one family and he asked if they had a daughter in Britain nursing.

They had.

Was her name Kathleen?

No, her name was Mary.

He described her and the family agreed it sounded like Mary. The family produced a photograph of Mary.

"That's her - that's Kathleen." He was jubilant. Then "Where is she - can I see her?"

"She's beyont in England married these two years."

3

CHAPTER ONE

Only then did he learn she had been christened Kathleen Mary and when in England had used her first Christian name as a nurse.

Fred de Vere slapped the story as the lead in the week-end sister paper, the *Ballina Herald*. The following day it made page one of the *Daily Mirror* which did not then circulate in Ireland; the clip was sent to me by friends in London. Fred de Vere himself cabled it to the *Sunday Independent* who made a Page One boxed story out of it. I wrote to the *Daily Mirror* claiming money for my exclusive story, to be told they got it from their local correspondent, Jack Reilly. Fred agreed he had sent it and would pay me out of the lineage cheque.

I used to go home to Charlestown each week-end to collect the news and notes there and in Swinford, the adjoining town. But I used also carry three dozen *Ballina Heralds* with me, trying to establish it in the region. They cost three shillings and nine pence in the old money. One Friday, Fred called me into his office. He had just got the lineage cheque and he'd got seven shillings and six-pence for the romance story.

"Now John more money for you this week". And he counted out the three shillings and ninepence very carefully. But before I could scoop it up he said ha-ha and smiled "you owe me three shillings and nine-pence for last week's *Heralds*. So that's the sixpence I owe you."

I had the rest of the evening to look at that sixpence and to smile ruefully. It represented three front page stories in two countries - tuppence a story!

Well now I had what I was sure was another front page story - only this time no one was going to 'milk' it or 'lift' it, or in plain language, pirate it. True, I had no correspondence and was unknown and unaccredited but before this night was out, I'd find some one, or some paper, in Fleet Street who'd buy it and ask no questions about accreditation.

HEALY, REPORTER

It was Press Night in the *Western People* , that long Wednesday night when the big Hoe Crabtree roared out the weekly paper. Reporters doubled up as counters, taking the papers from the feed-out. You tucked them under your arm and counted them off: three, six, nine, twelve; three, six, nine, twelve, dozen after dozen for three hours. Or more if you had a paper break.

There was another thing about press night: we were always broke. The reporters I mean. We might borrow a cigarette from one of the comps or the machine men, depending on the man's humour. On this particular press night we had paper breaks and I was broke so that when the run finished at two in the morning and Battle came over to me to see about his caption, I told him to come outside and I'd talk to him on his way home. I told him we were going to ring Fleet Street.

"That crowd won't take it - you have no correspondence."

"No - but we'll try someone."

The Daily Mail and the *Daily Express* both circulated in Ireland.

"But you don't have their numbers - how can you ring them?"

"I have no money either. Have you?"

"I only have half a crown."

"We'll toss to see which one we'll ring."

It came down heads for the *Daily Mail*.

The nice thing about a small market town like Ballina is that everyone knows everyone else and although I was a newcomer, I knew someone on the switchboard of the local post office. From the kiosk outside I made the call, explaining to the operator I had no money but would put it in the box on Friday and didn't know the number I wanted, but it was the *Daily Mail* .

"London or Manchester?"

I knew Fleet Street was in London, but Manchester was

nearer and cheaper and said Manchester. In a few seconds the
Daily Mail was on the line.

"Gimmie the newsdesk please." This, in what I hoped was
my best Bogart voice, at 2.30 in the morning.

"News desk here."

"I have an exclusive picture story here about Helen Hooker
O'Malley's third child."

"Yes old boy - what's the name?"

"Healy - I'm calling from Ballina in Mayo in Ireland."

"Spell it, old boy."

"Healy. HEALY BALLINA."

"Got it: Ballina." He put the emphasis on the last syllable.
Outside the box Battle has started to sweat: he sees me nodding
my head vigorously. I am giving the news desk the story and
he sticks his head in the door.

"Are they taking it?"

Vigorous silent nod, waving him away. He's back again.

"Get five pounds for it. It's worth a fiver."

I wave him away again.

At the other end of the phone the voice is excited,
"and you have the exclusive picture?"

"Nobody else got it."

"Fine old boy. Now when can you wire it to us?"

Battle is in again. "Get a fiver for it."

"Don't you want to talk a price first, old man?"

"So long as the picture is exclusive, old boy."

"I haven't called the *Express* - you have first refusal."

Battle's head is in again. He collects the back of my hand.

"Look old man, we'll pay you fifty pounds for the picture
exclusively."

"And twenty-five for the story?"

Battle hears only the last sentence. His head is in again:
"Don't kill it, don't kill it.

The voice at the other end: "All right, old boy.

Seventy-five for the story and picture exclusively. Now when can you wire it?"

"We can't."

Battle again misinterprets the single sentence and says: "Let him have it." This time I kept my hand on the handle of the kiosk to keep him out. I explain we have no wire machine this side of Dublin.

"OK old boy, fly it out."

We don't have an airport, except Shannon or Dublin."

"What do you have then?"

"We have a train leaving for Dublin at nine in the morning: it'll be there in the afternoon."

And that was it. We'd have it on the Dublin train and their staff photographer would pick it up and wire it to Manchester that evening. Battle, outside, was rubbing his hands: he knew the sale had been made. Old Boy thanked me again, took my full name and address and was about to hang up when I said:

"I may have a follow up - will you put me down as the *Mail's* accredited stringer here in Mayo?"

"Of course, Old Boy. Come through at any time."

Battle couldn't believe it. Never before had he got as much for a picture: was I sure it was pounds? I was sure. Now get that picture on the train in the morning...

Many years afterwards in New York I met Cormac O'Malley for the first time. It had been close on 27 years from the night of that phonecall to the *Daily Mail*. I said to him simply, "Cormac, you won't remember your first communion in Burrishoole - but it changed my luck, put me on my feet as a newspaperman and I've never looked back since."

Then I told him the story, and how I had started on the *Western People*, Ballina in the Summer of 1948.

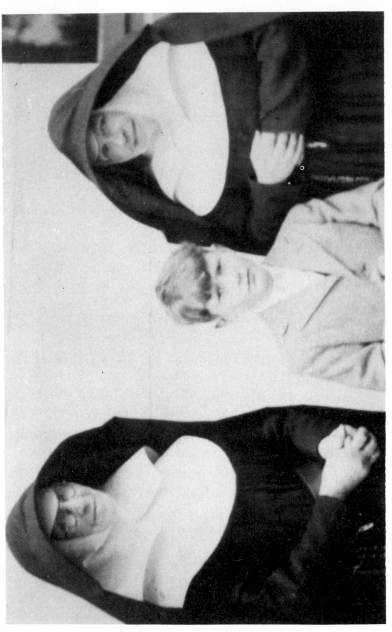

Reverend Mother Rose, Cormac O'Malley and Sr. Teresa, Convent of Mercy, Newport, Co. Mayo.   Photo: Mary Battle

TWO

My mother's ambition was that I would be a doctor. It was natural enough, for she was the district midwife and she knew the respect and financial status which a doctor had. There was a standing joke in our town that every time Dr. Michael Beirne, the local dispensary man, drove his Jaguar down the town it was costing someone two guineas. Half the town knew he had lost part of a fortune when Germany went to war: half his money, they said, was in Krupps of Germany.

I had my own very clear idea of what I wanted to do. I was going to be a newspaperman and nothing and no one would stop me.

In 1948 we didn't have much talk about career guidance or anything else, but even in National School I liked writing what we called grandly, 'compositions'.

It was in the diocesan secondary school, St. Nathy's, Ballaghaderreen, Co. Roscommon, that I met the first man to encourage me. I was 'streamed' in the 'B' class because my Irish and especially Maths were not up to the requirements for the Honours 'A' class. Professor William Reilly, popularly known as 'Billy' or 'Gosh', was the school's best known Maths teacher and he was tough as a teacher. We drew him for English in my first year. We all sweated through his first class.

He was very keen on poetry appreciation and after a few days he began to watch me. It was inevitable that, very

9

quickly, I was going to be the star pupil in the class though, in part, some of the class toughs weren't trying.

There was the day Billy wanted an appreciation on Joyce Kilmer's "Trees".

"All right, Haran - what had the poet in mind when he wrote 'a tree whose hungry mouth is prest, against the earth's sweet flowing breast'?"

Haran knew bloody well but he got up and stumbled out "I don't know sir."

"All right - sit down. You, Lang - what was the poet writing about?"

Lang wouldn't tell him either. He went through most of the class and, as the last man refused or didn't know, he exploded,

"Gosh - I suppose ye all think yer mothers found ye under a head of cabbage."

And then: "All right, Mister Healy - up on your legs and tell them".

"He is likening the earth to a mother's feeding breast, sir."

"Good man.. That'll do."

I had brought in a few essays to him and he was still not satisfied about something. Then one day he set us the task of writing, in class, an appreciation of a poem. It was the last class of a long, hot, summer's day and maybe he wanted to have an easy class. It didn't matter to me. I got out my exercise book and started writing at speed, once I had read the poem. Slowly, very slowly, I saw the shadow coming up behind me. First the head, then the shoulders. It stopped there and stood there until the end of the class, when he merely said: "All right - I'll collect them tomorrow".

As he passed me he put his hand on my shoulder and said:

"I wanted to see for myself" and went off.

Within the week I had got my rating. We were doing collective nouns and Billy was peppering us with questions:

10

What do you call a lot of geese? Badgers? Foxes? And then, pleased with the response from the class generally, he threw it out. "There is no one here who can tell me what you call a gathering of lions".

He looked sharply at me:

"It's called a pride, sir."

"Gosh, Healy you're a genius". He was openly amazed to find this in a 'B' class, and in First year.

But if I was a genius in Billy's eyes I was to pay heavily for it that long first year. As it happened he was teaching Honours English to the Leaving Certificate class that same year and before very long he was taking my essays up to that class to read them out as models of good writing.

Very shortly I was fair game for every Leaving class senior in the school. There was always one of them behind me in the daily trooping into or out of the refectory and they felt fully licensed to kick my backside when it presented itself. No one worked me over quite as hard as Charlie 'Tough' Gallagher of Cashel in Tubbercurry, the youngest of the famous Gallagher brothers who went on to be a millionaire in London in the 1970's. He was the only one of them, I believe, to get a secondary education.

Looking back I can understand it. After all, when you get a pedestrian title like 'A Day's Cycling' which gave most of the lads a lot to do to produce two pages of hand writing and this little skinny twirp from Charlestown - in a bloody 'B' class, to make things worse - came up with twenty-seven pages of fantastic adventures befalling him through the French countryside where an exploding tyre gets him picked up by the Maquis, he deserves his arse kicked. Billy was a bit more gentle, he merely scrawled across the last page: "Little man, You've Had a Busy Day".

When, in second year, we drew Billy for Maths, I dreaded it: the honeymoon would soon be over. I survived for a week

11

in his new class. Then, having posed a problem which the class failed to answer, he called on me to do the necessary. I couldn't.

"Gosh - a simple question like that."

"I'm not very good at Maths, sir."

Still puzzled, he told me to sit down, put another problem on the blackboard and came down to inquire what happened me? I explained I wasn't able to grasp Maths in the same way as English - there was no place for imagination as there was in English.

"But gosh, Maths is all imagination - that's why I thought you'd have no trouble."

I told him I didn't see it like that. Solicitously he asked:

"What are you going to do about your Intermediate Certificate...Maths is compulsory."

He was plainly concerned.

"I'm not worried about Maths, sir; for a living I'm going to be a newspaperman".

"Gosh" and his face lit up, "you're lucky. Good man yourself. You don't know how lucky you are to know now what you want to do. You will make a good journalist."

He could have walloped Maths into me like many another teacher, for every failure reflected on the teacher. But from that day till I left the school, Billy Reilly, inside or outside the classroom, not only exempted me from Maths but made time available to coach me privately in what I should be reading.

I was to be lucky with our second English teacher, Father Eugene Foran. He was a fine Shakespeare man and a fine analyst of English. He had a long and fruitful reign in St. Nathy's and one of his products was the great Joycean authority, John Garvin, later local appointments Commissioner in Dublin. Garvin was a pupil of his in the Twenties when Foran was pressing on them the newly

12

published work of Rupert Brooke and that of his contemporaries, the "War Poets".

We called him 'Mister'. He had a habit of saying "'Pon my word, mister" with every sentence but if he did he turned out generations of students with an appetite for Shakespeare which few others had. Foran's treatment of Shakespeare deserves a word. He came in first term and gave you the read in which he set the character values.

"'Pon my word, lads, you can't blame Harry Hotspur for not surrendering the prisoners. Here's this popinjay, mister, down from London, telling Harry the King wants the prisoners, mister and the battle's barely over. A popinjay, mister." Or "Now this man Falstaff, mister - a boon companion. Harry likes him - dammit all man, he knew one day he'd be king with a court around him. A stuffy court, mister - that's why he valued the company of Falstaff and the bawdy company." And he'd produce the relevant quotations to support the value he was giving the character. Which was fine until the second term when he started at the beginning again and you thought the old man was doddering.

So once again we came back to Hotspur and the issue of the prisoners. "No dammit, mister, Hotspur had no right to be short with the king's messenger. He was there because the king sent him - and the king is the king, mister. It's no use saying Hotspur is hot-blooded - the king is the king, mister, and must be obeyed in all things."

Foran had a great habit of pretending to be deaf and when some of the class mimics started to imitate him he paid no apparent attention. So from half way down the classroom you'd hear,

"You're only a daft ould bollocks, mister, you were all for Hotspur last year."

Foran wouldn't pretend to hear. "Now this Falstaff, mister, he's really a low type. A scrounger, mister. Think of

13

the scandal - a future ruler going round the taverns with this pot-bellied dirty old man."

"You're only an ould bollocks yerself, Foran."

He would stop to signal he had heard it but would say nothing.

"Where were we? Yes, Falstaff. Now it's no use Hotspur telling us that he's going to sink down to all the depravities of low life, mister, so that when he reforms, his reformation will make him shine in a new light. That's deceit, mister, deceit."

Gradually it dawned on you, Foran was reversing completely the values he had given you for each character the previous term - and was supporting the new "read" from the same text. Nothing he said could be contradicted: he was producing irrefutable evidence out of each character's mouth to sustain these new interpretations. Very soon you realised the passages you glossed over last term as rhetorical flourishes had indeed a very different significance and importance. For me it was, once I saw where he was going, such an excitement that I started to comb the text looking for likely passages he would quote as he went through the term but, more importantly, looking to see if I could pull from the totality of the text yet a third interpretation of the main characters.

In the end I came to the conclusion that Shakespeare was not only a great man with words - he was also the world's first psychologist. Foran's talent for taking the written word and examining it from every possible angle was something which would be very useful on the Press Gallery of Dáil Éireann many years later when Lynch-speak was to become the political language of the day in the turbulent time when the North of Ireland erupted making life very difficult for the third leader of the Fianna Fáil Republican Party.

That was a long way in the future and now, finished in school to my own satisfaction and despite my mother's contrary ambition, I had to get a start in a local paper. A school pal, 'Meehaul' Campbell of Swinford, suggested the *Mayo News* and writing to them.

I decided the usual formal application would be no use. It should have a sample story included with it to show what I could do. John McIntyre had just opened a new Cola plant in Charlestown and I thought I should go and see it and interview him. I went into Honan's and bought a copy book. It was Fair Day and I bumped into Paddy Kenny, a neighbour, in my rush out the door.

"What has you in such a hurry?"

"See that copy-book, Paddy - that's going to make me my living. I'm starting to be a reporter."

And I was off.

I described the new plant and gave the background of its owner. The story ran to about one thousand words. I knew even then that the last sentence should have a bit of punch - or what we later called "the punchline". So it had. It went like this: "Mr. McIntyre said as I was leaving 'Remember, young Healy, we don't stock the best - we sell it'."

For ten days I heard nothing. Then a nice polite letter came back with the story. It said the paper had no vacancies. The Editor had read the story "and it shows a lot of promise". That wasn't enough for me. Next I would try the *Western People* in Ballina, thirty miles away - but this time I would go in person and talk the editor into giving me a job. More correctly, write my way into a job.

I imagined myself in the editor's office. I sat down and wrote "The young man sitting across the desk from you is John Healy. He wants to be a reporter..."

And on it went giving what is today called a profile of myself. That was the first letter. The second letter I would hand him would be the McIntyre story and I would wait impatiently while The Great Man read it. I could wait for the approval coming across the big flat polished desk that editors always had. . .

I have told in another place the story of that day, smuggling out my best suit, borrowing a neighbour's bike, finally getting to Ballina to be told by the manager that I could clear home to hell - they didn't want any reporters; and of waiting until five in the evening when I knew the editor would be in his office.

Fred de Vere was a big man. He was big in physique, he had a big bulbous nose which looked incongruous beside the rosebud he always wore in his lapel. His office was a dump, dusty and mouldy, and there was no big polished desk but a roll-top bureau heaped with papers. There was no chair. I had to stand beside him. He read the profile. Then I handed him the story, feeling a lot less certain now. He read it, his Parker pen making paragraph signs as if he were sub-editing it.

"Never say 'he concluded by saying': 'he concluded' is enough." That was all the fault he had to find in it. There followed a long spiel about the long waiting list which he had; how well all the young men who had come through his hands had done; he had trained the best men in Dublin journalism today and once it was known you were a trainee of the *Western People* you would qualify for a job in any part of the world. Did I have shorthand? No, but I intended learning it. Good. He was the fastest shorthand note-taker in Ireland, he told me. He was the only man capable of taking a good note of some fast-talking politician he named. I was suitably impressed. He could take me on as a trainee reporter but I would have to live in Ballina.

"That will be no trouble, sir"

"Normally our trainees have shorthand and typing and they start at ten shillings a week but they live here at home in Ballina."

"I can live in Ballina, sir".

16

"Yes, well, I can give you a pound a week to start."

He looked up at me and then, in what I was later to realise was a tremendous burst of beaming generosity, added "And I'll put the stamp on your card for you. You can start on Monday."

I would have to fight my mother yet, but I knew then I was on my way.

THREE

In the last quarter of the Twentieth Century, when trainee reporters start at something like five thousand pounds a year, to say you were happy to get fifty-two pounds a year makes you sound like something out of Dickens and the Nineteenth Century, yet that was the scale of pay in the *Western People* in 1948. You had to be in love with newspapers to do it - and I was in love with newspapers.

Still the question remains: how to live on one pound a week and pay two pounds five shillings for digs, not to mention eight shillings for the busfare home and back to Ballina on the week-end? The fact of the matter is that you didn't.

My mother opposed the idea of a career in newspapers. I would return to school and finish my education by sitting the Leaving Certificate and, hopefully, go on to be a doctor. That the family hadn't the money to make me a doctor didn't seem to have occurred to her - unless it was that she hoped her American sisters would finance it. The idea of a career which wasn't pensionable doubly appalled her.

"What are you going to do in your old age with no pension?"

I had enough self-confidence to reply: "I'll be so famous by then that one article a week will earn me enough".

I never had any doubts but that I would be 'famous'. Anyway, I argued, if you force me back to St. Nathy's, I'll still want to be a newspaperman when I finish: I will still have to start at one pound a week - so why not give me the college fee towards my upkeep in Ballina where, after two years, I will be earning a bit more? Indeed, with any luck, I might even be self-sufficient. My father supported the argument and she capitulated reluctantly. And so I was subsidised by thirty shillings a week with my father slipping me the odd pound note maybe every third week. My arrangement with the landlady was a vital part of the financing: we agreed that she would be paid monthly in arrears. It was to have one disastrous repercussion later on but at first it gave me a breathing space.

My first assignment out of the office was to my hometown of Charlestown to cover the annual agricultural show. Fred de Vere explained that the normal press facilities would be provided by the Committee. These included two catalogues on which to mark the results and a lunch voucher.

I presented myself to the Show secretary Tommy Murphy and asked for the usual press facilities. What did I mean?

"The traditional two catalogues and a lunch voucher."

"You can buy two catalogues - and if you have to eat you can go down home and eat."

I told him these were the traditional courtesies extended to the Press and I was entitled to them: if he was not providing them then my paper would say so and we would not carry a report of the show. As far as he was concerned I could f**k off - a bloody little upstart. I said fine and contacted my colleagues from the other local papers. I had been refused the facilities and I proposed the show should therefore be blacked. They agreed.

I returned to Ballina, wrote a short paragraph to say that because of the refusal of the usual press facilities we regretted we could not carry the results of the Charlestown Show, and handed it in to the editor. I explained the encounter with Mr. Murphy.

"Quite right" said Fred, who always had a very proper regard for the professional dignity of the calling.

When the paper came out, there was murder in Charlestown. The Show Committee met in session and Mr. Murphy was directed to write a letter saying Mr. Healy had full facilities to report the show. The letter was published in full. I came back the following week and detailed the exchanges between Mr. Murphy and myself. Mr. Murphy came back the third week and put his efficiency as secretary to the Show Committee on the line and further, his efficiency as secretary of the Town Hall Committee, implying his was a better track record than young Mr. Healy's.

By now the controversy was a news story in itself and the town was rather enjoying the set to, between young Healy and the older Murphy who had maybe ten years on me.

It was rank bad luck that the week Tommy, who was in truth a very brilliant lad whose talent never had a chance to flourish in the town, enlarged the controversy by throwing in his secretaryship of the Town Hall, should be the very week-end when a band he had booked failed to turn up! I was passing the Town Hall and saw the crowd milling around and was told:

"Murphy forgot to book a band".

Someone else added: "And he booked two bands the one night three months ago".

Week Four and the botched band bookings kept the pot boiling and Tommy was back again, this time explaining about the bands and the original issue of the show facilities was now forgotten. Fred thought enough was enough. He appended a footnote to Tommy's last letter. This correspondence is now closed: we prefer to take the word of our Mr. Healy whom we know than of Mr. Murphy whom we have not the pleasure of knowing.

I had, without knowing it, come through my baptism as a

cub and I was very impressed with the way Fred de Vere stood behind me so publicly. Fred de Vere was a magnificent editor and a miserable employer. At that time he and his brother, Vincent, owned the paper between them. Vincie was a manager of sorts. I say 'of sorts' because it is very doubtful just what role he played in Fred's hey-day: they would fight in front of the staff and Fred, shouting, would dismiss Vincie as a madman. Vincie, later, would assure us that he didn't know what got into Fred at times.

Fred would be in first in the morning. He went through the post, ripping open each envelope in search of the cheques, discarding 'no-money' letters to one side until he had dealt with the money. When Fred was handling money he was impervious to everything else. He would get bills paid by pound notes and fivers: cheques were few and if it wasn't cash it was money orders or postal orders. Fred divided the cash from the money orders. The money orders he put in a Gold Flake tobacco box: he had another box for the cash. Once, as he had finished the morning's segregation, I told him two Sisters of Charity were at the counter. He insisted on putting the money into its boxes, opening the big safe and locking it away before attending to the sisters. That morning ritual was such, as I say, that you could be standing beside him and relaying a message but he simply did not hear you. Tony Bourke and Aidan Hennigan, now London Editor of the *Irish Press*, one Monday morning tried in vain to gain his attention. I bet each of them a shilling I'd gain it. Fred's office was a remarkable affair but it had a window opening out on to the works and the reporters' bench was directly under his gaze so that when I went in to try where they had failed, they could clearly see both of us.

"Sir?" I said, standing beside him, watching his fingers ripping open the letters and fishing out the money.

No reply. I had half a crown in my pocket, took it out

and, sliding out the leaf for note-taking, hopped the half-crown off it.

"Yes, John, yes, yes - what is it?"

The sound, no less than the sight, of money was always too much for Fred. The boys paid up reluctantly: they argued I had cheated.

Fred de Vere was his own editor, his own proof reader, his own cashier and accountant and promotions manager into the bargain. He proof read every line of his paper, small ads and all. We had to hold copy for him, reading out the original advertisement while he read the proof. He sent out monthly accounts and we read copy on them, too. When the account was a month overdue, we learned to hand it to him and he scrawled across it with his Parker pen "Please remit promptly", never lifting the pen from the paper so that all three words ran on. Reporters were also expected to type the wrappers for individual subscribers and stamp them and double up as stenographers to Fred.

With Fred, who was big framed and over six foot in height, work was a pleasure. He did so much there was nothing for Vincie to do. If Vincie ordered reporters around, Fred countermanded it. Poor Vincie had only one man he could boss - and that man was straight out of Dickens. He was Paddy Guinan and I suppose he might be called the advertising manager in another day. In fact, with Vincie bellowing at him - "God blast ye to hell, Guinan - what's keeping you?" - Paddy entered in big old ledgers the names of small ad customers, box numbers and the price and number of insertions. He did likewise for the space bookings. He worked in the old *Ballina Herald* office while the main works was in Francis Street: the connection was by phone. Paddy Guinan was thin and gaunt. His collar was too big and his hair was thin and straggly. His coat was so big that when he scurried up from Garden Street to head office it seemed to be flying in

22

tails behind him. Unseen devils in the form of Vincie's blasting voice appeared to drive him.

That man took dog's abuse from Vincie and only once did he ever choke Vincie off - and even today none of who witnessed it can be sure it was deliberate. Vincie would ring down to Garden Street where there was an exchange which Paddy Guinan used to put calls through to head office. Vincie lit the air blue when he was in good form and poor Guinan had long learned that you never interrupted the harangue. Vincie was in top gear, riding poor Guinan from a height and the shouting was positively sulphurous until, of a sudden, it stopped and Vincie pulled the phone away from his ear to look at it in some disbelief. Next we heard him say,

"Yes your Lordship, of course your Lordship".

I would not think Dr. Patrick O'Boyle, Bishop of Killala, was a stranger to the vocabulary but he certainly had a full minute of Vintage Vincie to refresh his memory...

The paper was a family affair, as are most provincial papers in Ireland. In the lino room was Fred's brother and two nephews. Fred's brother, Ernie, called himself Devers and the legend in Ballina was that the true family was Devers but when Fred took over he and Vincent became known as De Veres. Ernie was not merely a lino-man: he was also the nearest thing to a sub-editor we had in my time.

Fred let you write. You could go two thousand words on a football match and that was fine by Fred. Ernie, on the other hand, had to set the copy and being a good Gaelic player in his day, would spot inconsistencies in a young reporter's copy. He'd shuffle up in his slippers, the eternal fag in his mouth, and ask you

"What kind of shit is this?" Fred had read it and passed it - now here was a bloody lino man querying it. But very soon I learned to listen to Ernie and to watch the way he made cuts avoiding repetitions.

CHAPTER THREE

Fred and Vincie might fight like cats but no one ever fought with Ernie or his sons. They, on the other hand, deplored the family fights in front of the staff.

Fred was never slow in promoting his paper. At very regular intervals the readers would be told that it was the biggest provincial paper in Ireland and the weekly newsprint it used came in reels which, if placed end to end would stretch from Belmullet to Longford. It had the highest paid staff in the country and the biggest staff as well. Now that was fine as a piece of flak but it caused me personally a lot of distress. Living in Charlestown and going to Sunday Mass where you were expected to contribute to the Christmas and Easter collections, and Fr. Eddie O'Hara, the Parish Priest, reading that you were part of the highest paid staff in provincial journalism, expected something more than two shillings on the plate. When I mentioned this to Fred in trying to get an increase, he told me I needn't go home on such collection days - I could always duck in to the Cathedral where no one would notice me. How he expected me to bring back two columns of Charlestown notes on such week-ends was something he never explained!

For all of that, I made out. Christmas came but there was no Christmas Bonus. That first Christmas in Ballina was saved for me when Frank McCormack, a jeweller friend I had made in the F.C.A., gave me a new Golmet pen as a present.

With no spare money my social life was curtailed in that first six months. In the digs there would be an odd game of penny poker to pass a night and the landlady would sit in sometimes. One night I decided to sit in: I had five shillings to spare. As the night wore on it became a sixpenny game and the betting got heavier. I had my landlady's money in my pocket: I was to pay her the following day. The last pot of the night was a two shilling 'chuck' - everyone posted two shillings to start. There were several good hands out and the 'kitty' was

24

worth five pounds after the first round of bets. I had four aces, than which there is no better hand. But to the right and left of me were two men with very good hands and they kept raising each other with me caught in the middle. Johnny would raise it by a pound: I, next to him, would 'see' him but Joe would raise it again, whereupon Johnny would raise it again and I would 'see'. In the end I was out of money and I asked for credit. No credit. Cash only. Pay up or throw in your hand. I had no option. The landlady watched the duel between the two. They finally put there cards on the table. I turned up the hand I was forced to discard - they were full of sympathy but that was the luck of the game.

The landlady knew her rent money was gone and for my indiscretion she made her displeasure known next morning when, at breakfast, she whipped the butter dish from under my nose and slapped down margarine. I was to stay in the margarine dog-house until the night Tommy Battle produced his first communion picture of Cormac O'Malley and we were paid our exclusive fee and expenses by the *Daily Mail*. I told Tommy about the margarine and an elated Tommy said:

"Why don't you come down and stay with us - we have a spare room."

I discharged my debt and moved down to Tommy and Mary and I was happy there. Tommy was happy too, for he had a built-in caption writer in the house and there was always a chance we might bring off another coup.

Battle suited me as much as I suited Battle and he had a library of pictures going back over the years. I learned now what year it was that Tommy took a picture of the Moy in flood at Foxford, showing the fields covered with flood waters. But every winter, regular as clockwork, Tommy hauled out the negative, ran up four prints of it and sent it off to the three Dublin dailies and the *Cork Examiner*. Just as regularly the papers printed them. Long years afterwards in

CHAPTER THREE

Dublin I'd see Battle's hardy annual picture used again and again. There was no man sorrier than Tommy when they drained the Moy and put an end to the flood waters at Foxford! He was luckier with a picture of an old lady he photographed with a hay rake in her hand beside a cock of hay. She was in her early eighties when he first published the picture of Mrs Catherine Leonard of Lahardane helping with the hay. The woman lived into her nineties and every year, making a check call to see she was still alive, she kept on appearing, helping with the hay.

Tommy gave me a few bob whenever a picture with my caption appeared, and I realised that since Fred de Vere wasn't going to showers riches on me, there was a dire need to get accredited as correspondent to some of the other papers. I had the *Daily Mail* which automatically included the *Sunday Dispatch*. *Daily Mail* stories were thin enough in Ballina but the *Sunday Dispatch* was another matter. It seemed to have a whole page of Irish news. I studied the sort of stories they printed. They were generally five hundred words, light and off-beat. Many of them were about towns or villages "up in arms" about something or other. "Up in arms" seemed to be the in-thing. Then there was the "only-woman" story. Or "Ireland's oldest woman water-diviner" or "Ireland's youngest".

I was still looking for the "onlies" or the "up in arms" people when the *Times Pictorial* in Dublin advertised for local correspondents who would submit five hundred word stories of an amusing or off-beat nature. Two of us applied from Ballina and I lost. But I saw the detailed circular sent to Jim McGuire outlining the requirements. It boiled down to this: if you could write a story with a good catchy headline you were there. The editor, George Burrows, in turning me down said he could not have two men in one district. All right - so Jim McGuire would cover Ballina. I would cover East Mayo. The way to do it would be to get a story and send it in with a renewed application.

At that time there was a great market in Britain for Irish rabbits and the most effective way was to dazzle them with the dynamo lamp of a bicycle. To power it you had to turn the wheel, forcing you to carry the frame of the bike on your shoulder. It was awkward and a few of us got to thinking as to how we could drive the dynamo without humping the bicycle frame round; we wanted something more portable. We decided we'd try one of the old fashioned wind-up gramophones, running the dynamo off the turntable. That was it! I had my headline.

"THEY CATCH RABBITS - BY GRAMOPHONE!"

I picked up the *Times Pictorial* the following week - and there it was. George agreed to me doing East Mayo - and ever story was half a guinea. Riches untold! Within a month I had three front page stories - worth five pounds each - with photographs by the late Dermot Barry and a warm letter of appreciation from George Burrows. George Burrows and the now defunct *'Times Pic'* as we called it, kept my head above water, for hardly a week passed but I had one, if not two, stories in it. In fact, wherever I went, whatever I heard, I was constantly turning it around in my mind, looking for 'the angle', or that one tag line for a heading which, I knew, would carry the story and make me half a guinea.

You didn't have any option. You were hungry and you had to survive and a half guinea was a fortune in the week.

But there was more to it than that - there was the great exciting element of competition because you were competing for limited space with every other news man in Ireland. Holding your own against them - that was every bit as important as the half guineas.

It helped to have stars in your eyes, too...

FOUR

I was supposed to learn shorthand and become a proficient typist. After the first few weeks, when I lost interest in Pitman exercises and Fred didn't seem to mind, I was producing columns of copy without it and picking them out on the battered office typewriter. I was to pay for not learning shorthand, for when I sought an increase Fred asked for my shorthand speed and I didn't have any. There was no increase until I was there for a year when I got a half a guinea on top of the pound.

But if Fred de Vere was tight with the money he did give us something far more valuable: we had all the space in the world in which to write. You could write your head off and everything went into the paper. Sometimes, to your astonishment, in the oddest places.

The Summer of 1948 was one of football fever in Mayo. Our senior team was in the All-Ireland final with Cavan. It was our first chance of bringing the Sam Maguire Cup home since the heady days of 1936. At that time teams went in for collective training and the Mayo Team was billeted in my digs. No one will ever know the privilege it was for a youngster who had worshipped these men from afar to find himself actually living with them, getting up and going to bed with the powerful aroma of wintergreen, listening at the breakfast and lunch table as they talked about the coming match. Aidan Hennigan, who was primarily a Rugger man, was the Gaelic correspondent and at the best of times he hadn't much heart for it. On the week-end of the final I was so carried away with the fever that I sat down and wrote a piece in which I was Micheal O'Hehir, broadcasting the last ten minutes of the match on Radio Éireann.

It had the lot, the solo run by Sean Mulderrig, the brilliant passing movements between Peter Solan and Tom Acton and the pile-driving goal by Tom Langan, the raw-boned man from Ballycastle. Now there was only a point in it and the time was ticking away.

Well, naturally Mayo equalised and then went on in the dying kick of the game to score a point to take the Cup. I dropped it in Fred's basket. When I next saw it, it was the lead story in the *Ballina Journal*, our week-end paper, with a clatter of straplines and headlines written by Fred himself.

"Could I go to Dublin to the match, sir?"

"Certainly not. Aidan is covering it. You are to be in this office at nine on Monday morning."

It was a death blow. After the weeks of living and sleeping and eating with this great Mayo team I was not to see them play the greatest game of all.

Hennigan told me not to worry: he'd organise a lift for me. I was only a month in the paper at this time and knew no one in Ballina. A lift with the team was impossible but Aidan assured me I'd be OK - he'd get a lift to Dublin for me.

Saturday afternoon came and Hennigan's lift never appeared. The cars were heading out from Ballina, red and green flags flying and everyone of them stuffed with supporters. I damned Hennigan and Fred de Vere and the whole miserable world from a height and was venting my rage 'butting' stones on the Court House wall when the proprietor of the American Bar, next door to my digs, asked what was up with me. He saw the tears in my eyes and when I told him I couldn't get a lift to Dublin, he said: "I'm leaving in five minutes - I'll squeeze you in, but I'm not coming back till Tuesday".

"Great, I'll be with ye."

Half an hour later I was on my way to Dublin City for the first time. I didn't know how I'd get back to Ballina by Monday morning and just now it could wait: my biggest task was to get into Croke Park tomorrow and see Mayo win this All-Ireland Final.

I was so preoccupied with that thought it never occurred to me to think of where I was going to spend the night - and all I had was Fred de Vere's precious pound note and a two shilling piece.

"Where are you staying?" John Walsh asked me.

"Drop me at Barry's Hotel."

That was where the Mayo Team was staying. Barry's was thronged with people all milling round on the steps outside trying to get in. Half of Mayo, it seemed, was trying to push in the doors - and the other half trying to get out. Among the Mayo people trying to force a way out as I was trying to get in was Tom Lanagan, whom I had described as "the raw-boned man from Ballycastle". He caught sight of me going towards him and let fly with a straight right hand. The fist crunched on the bridge of my nose. A priest beside him restrained him from anything further. "Now who's raw-boned?" he shot back as he was bundled away. Someone asked me if he hurt me and I said no, not at all. The Charlestowners and Swinfords were all over the place. A few were going for a meal and invited me to join them. That looked after that meal. Around midnight the crowd began to thin out. Fr. Paddy Towey, longtime member of the Mayo County Board and a teacher of mine in St. Nathy's inquired if I had a bed for the night. I hadn't, I said. Barry's was full. A friend from home joined us and Paddy said I hadn't a bed. "Not to worry" said my friend, there was a spare bed in his digs. I could have it.

My friend was celebrating in advance and by the time we set out on foot for his digs he was 'nicely'. I had no idea where we were after half an hour's walking. He stopped and wagged a finger at me:

"Stay here for a minute until I see if the coast is clear - she's a bit of a barge".

He was fumbling a long time with the key when the door opened and the barge appeared: she did not approve of her guest rolling home drunk. That was enough for me: I faded into the shadows of the trees. It was a warm and close September night and I didn't mind.

I tried a few parked cars: they were all locked. Down a sidestreet I saw a lorry. The door was open and I climbed in. Now the dangers of being alone in a strange city started to gnaw at my mind - strangers were often attacked and beaten for their money. Not that I had much money - but you never knew. Where would I hide the pound note so that they wouldn't get it if they searched me? Five minutes later I peeled off my left shoe and stocking and put the pound note under the sole of my foot, drew on the stocking and shoe and my mind was easier.

I was just settling into a sleep of sorts when, from the house beside me a couple started to argue. It was very obviously a husband and wife having a good barney. Between them and the all pervasive smell of sheep skins on the back of the lorry I slept very little and at first light I was away, looking for Barry's.

I hadn't the slightest idea where it was other than it was near O'Connell Street. Yes, but what direction was O'Connell Street? I saw tram tracks - that was it! Follow the tram tracks and you had to get to O'Connell Street. I was walking for half an hour before it occurred to me that the tram tracks could be leading away from Nelson's Pillar as well as to it. The buses hadn't started to run. A woman obviously hurrying to an

31

CHAPTER FOUR

early Mass gave me what seemed complicated instructions but I had the right direction on the tram tracks now: follow them and I had to hit O'Connell Street.

I noticed the neon signs. The really big ones flashed red and green, the Mayo colours. Clever of the traders, I thought, to have the flashing signs in the great red and green to gull the country fellows. (It would be a few years afterwards I'd appreciate that they were the great contrasting colours favoured in advertising in neon).

Back at Barry's I met the crowd from home, specifically 'Meehaul' Campbell of Swinford and his sister Maureen who was my first girl-friend. They had a big basket of sandwiches: we'd try early for Hill Sixteen and we'd have lunch. I told Meehaul I was stuck for a lift home.

"Don't worry: eight of our busload are going to England tonight: we have spare seats and you can be home with us."

Better still, the bus had to return to its depot in Ballina, so I would make it back to Ballina to be in time for work on Monday morning. At the entrance gate I showed my press card: "John J. Healy *Western People* Staff Reprepresentative". Fred 'togged' us out with identity cards. It is the one and only time in my life I carried a card. Croke Park honoured it. Did I want to go on the stand? No, I was to cover the match from behind the goal at Hill Sixteen. I wouldn't be behind the goal on the Hill, he said. Well, that's where I was supposed to be. Alright Meehaul and his friends followed me so that we all stuck together . . .

Being the goalkeeper for our own local Charlestown Sarsfields Team, Tom Byrne, the Mayo goalie, was my particular hero and here I was, right behind the net, waiting for the throw-in. I had my breakfast-cum-lunch from the Campbell basket but the excitement was too much and the food wasn't that important now . . .

And then our lads were on the field, fit and trim, Carney

banging the ball, Mongey returning it, Solan making a burst to send a high ball to Peter Quinn, big Pad MacAndrew, huge bacon hands, raking the clouds for a ball: he was the tallest man on the field, the giant from Erris. The march past with the Artane Boy's Band, The Soldiers' Song sending nerves of pride tingling up and down the spine until, last line lost in the huge cheers, the band hurried off the field, the whistle went and the game was on.

No Mayoman who was in Croke Park on that fatal final in 1948 will ever forget that match, live though he will to be a hundred. There was only one team in that first half and that was Cavan. I died three awful deaths in that first half when Tom Byrne, utterly and completely unnerved, let three soft goals in the back of the net, One, incredibly, went through his legs - I was there, I tell you, right behind him. I couldn't have been more ashamed had I been in his place. It was unbelievable - hadn't we all seen him stopping blinders in the games up to now, pouncing like a cougar on angled balls shot from ten yards.

We were in desolation at half time. The score-board was Cavan 3-2: Mayo 0-0.

Mayo wasn't even 'mapped' as we'd say. And then the second half came - and Mayo came storming back. Carney and Mongey clicked into gear and now our forwards were getting the ball. One goal, then another, and Cavan was under pressure. Byrne was now at the far end of the field, the Canal End and Des Benson was goal keeper for Cavan. Byrne played great in the second half and now it was Benson's turn, in the Cavan goal, to be humiliated. He stopped several shots but the Mayo pressure was relentless now and in a goal mouth melee Tom Acton and Tom Langan tumbled the ball over the line. With a brace of points, the two teams were now level going into the last five minutes. Cavan were attacking at the far end and Sean Flanagan came out to intercept Mick Higgins on the left wing. Flanagan simply pulled him down cleanly in a clear foul. It was coldly calculated. The wind was against Cavan: a shot from that position was difficult. But the wind coming off the stand curled the ball over the Mayo bar for a point lead.

Well, there was four minutes in it yet and the Mayo team came storming back. In front of me a Franciscan priest who had started reading his office from his breviary - and he must have been praying for Mayo - had it still open, except now he'd look up when the Mayo cheers rang out. Now Mayo came charging downfield and Peter Quinn was positioned dead between the posts of the Cavan goal, solo-running the ball, the forwards moving up with him.

The whistle went. The pain which flashed across Quinn's face I can still see. He looked at the referee, as if asking what foul he had committed. But the ref called for the ball - it was, incredibly, all over. The Franciscan said plaintively: "Fuck that" and slammed his breviary closed. All around that stadium the Mayo supporters checked their watches again and refused to believe what was happening - there was four minutes to go to full time.

We were robbed.

And we were - utterly and simply robbed. The controversy would grow in the following months and years and this would be known as the short-half All-Ireland and would rival the long count in the Dempsey/Tunny boxing match. Croke Park executives would acknowledge the robbery by installing the Bogue clock later which we in Mayo took as an act of reparation for that robbery. Cavan got the game and Mayo the glory for that magnificent fight back.

I left Croke Park crying that day but soon the tears dried when I had a vision of Fred looking for me if I missed the bus. It was parked at Aston Quay and we streamed down O'Connell Street, our flags furled, crestfallen. The Cavan supporters were jubilant.

The passengers were slow in arriving and it was almost seven in the evening when we were ready to leave for Mayo. Some of them were 'nicely' having drowned their sorrows in a few of the pubs on the way. Someone said we should check we had everyone and that we weren't missing anyone. A count was made. Thirty-three. That's right said someone, we had forty coming up and the rest went to England - go on, start her up. Wait a minute, if we had forty coming up and eight went to England - that doesn't add up. Count them again. They counted again, Campbell telling me not to worry. We have thirty-three.

You should only have thirty-two. The voice was that of John Egan, the Swinford publican. There's someone on the bus not entitled to be. John stumbled to the top of the bus and wove his way down, peering at everyone, checking the name. He came across me, asked my name and before I could answer it Meehaul Campbell had said:

"Look, its all right John - he's a young newspaperman from home and I told him we'd give him a lift".

But John was in an argumentative mood. The rest paid, there was no reason I shouldn't. I was ready to abandon the bus when Meehaul argued with John again. I was a school pal of his. I had a lift but he asked me to come with them: he knew there would be empty seats.

John, the fumes of the alcohol getting to him more and more, argued thickly and said I'd have to pay one way or another. focussing on me he asked:

"Can you sing?"

"I can."

"Well sing - now."

I sang 'I'm looking over a four leaf clover' and when I finished it John said:

"Sing it again."

CHAPTER FOUR

The bus, finally, pulled away and John was seated behind me. I didn't mind now: we were on our way home. But John did. Every time I finished that chorus, John, his voice, like his body, sinking lower in the seat, always managed "again". The bus joined in with me for the first fifteen miles and it was outside Mullingar that John finally succumbed to the sleep. The next morning, absolutely voiceless, I presented myself in time for work. Fred could say nothing. There was a collection for the driver and I contributed one shilling. I was to make dearer trips to Dublin later.

In 1949 every sports writer in the country tipped Mayo to win the All-Ireland Final. All but one. Me. I said Meath would beat them in the semi-final and would do it by hitting our light forwards hard in the opening quarter: that our forwards would overcarry the ball instead of taking their points from outfield.

Meath beat us in the semi-final. It was the poorest of comforts to be the only one to have it right, and no-one thanked me for it. The following year again, in 1950, I picked the team in February I held would win the All-Ireland if the selectors had the wisdom to agree with me. Thirteen of that team lined out for the All-Ireland final the following September: before the hour was out the two other players I had named were brought on.

This time we came home in triumph. Cocks of hay were fired as the train passed over the Mayo border and all along the line the people cheered. In Castlebar the heroes were welcomed with bonfires and blazing sods on hay forks.

Mayo went mad that night. The victory dinner in Castlebar was packed. The tomato soup was set down at the Press Table when some official of the County Board came up and inquired if I was "Kipper", the pen-name under which I wrote G.A.A. commentaries.

I said "Yes".

"Get Out".

I protested. So did some of my colleagues from the local and national press. But it was useless.

I was ejected. A score had been settled. The previous year I had mounted a campaign against dirty play and was supported in it by some of the County players. One Mayo star gave me evidence of how, in the 1948 final, he was instructed to "sort out" a Cavan star and when he refused to obey was told to "lie down" and come off the field. He refused and was switched and the Cavan man was indeed "sorted out". There had been a lot of dirty play in Mayo G.A.A. games and I documented cases of injured players.

The Mayo County Board was called into emergency session to consider the charges and ended the meeting with a solicitor's letter to the *Western People* charging libel. Fred called me in:

"Well John, you're in the wars" and showed me the letter.

I gave him my sources.

"Will they stand with you in Court?" Fred asked.

I went back to the players. Yes, they would go into a witness box and substantiate the charges. I told Fred.

"Take a letter" he said.

It was short and sweet: the paper would reiterate the charges the following week, after which the County Board could feel free to nominate their solicitors. We would defend the action. The County Board refused to take up the challenge. Instead they passed a resolution banning "Kipper" from all G.A.A. parks and games in Connaught.

Years later when I came to Dublin and became a very close friend of the late Padraig Ó Caoimh, General Secretary of the G.A.A. he told me the Mayo County Board had written to him about the affair and the wisdom of pressing the action or not. Padraig told them if they were blameless they should by all means press the action. If on the other hand there was substance in the allegations they would do well to attend to the matter and rectify the position.

So Castlebar settled the score. Half a dozen fairly prominent supporters who witnessed the ejection protested and refused to take their seats.

I had my own say the next week and got a fair amount of support from readers. But it didn't really matter to me. Mayo had won the Sam Maguire Cup and I was there to see it and to come home with it. It would be the first of many journeys with that same cup and I would always be a welcome guest...

MAYO SENIOR FOOTBALL TEAM 1948

Front Row: T Beirne, B Kenny, P Solan, S Flanagan, P Carney, J Forde, P Quinn, T Langan, P Prendergast, M Flanagan. **Back Row:** F Mongey, J Carney, J Gilvarry, E Mongey, P Jordan, S Daly, H Dixon, T Acton, Pop McNamera, Joe Gilvarry, S Mulderrig, L Hastings, P Gilvarry: Pat McAndrew, G Courell, J Munnelly, P Conway.

Photo: *Irish Press*

Aidan 'Taxi' Hennigan

FIVE

It had to be Wednesday.

Aidan Hennigan, known to all as 'Taxi', and myself were returning after lunch to the office in Francis Street. Hennigan had just lit a full cigarette.

This, to me, was most comforting: on Wednesday reporters simply didn't have the money for full cigarettes unless there had been a windfall of some kind. Windfalls were so rare I can remember them yet, all three of them in two years!

What was comforting about Taxi having a full cigarette was this: by the time we arrived at the office he would have reached the butt - and I was in line for the precious butt.

Coming down the sidewalk, against us, was Micksie Murphy. Micksie was one of the town's top five businessmen, local bank director and leading member of the Ballina Rugby Club.

When he was within twelve yards of us, coming towards us, Taxi took the cigarette from his lips, poised it between index finger and thumb, and then catapulted it into a gentle arc so that it landed a foot or two in front of Micksie.

I swear to this day that Micksie Murphy almost tripped over it. He certainly broke his stride and looked down at the smouldering full cigarette. By now we were almost level with him and, it seemed, before he had time to recover, Taxi called out cheerfully

"Great day, Micksie".

41

CHAPTER FIVE

And so we passed each other. I said nothing. I would wait until we reached the office to bone Taxi for a cigarette. A phone had to be answered as soon as we got there and I answered it. I was just settling down to type up a paragraph when Taxi came over.

"Have you any butts, Healy?"

I was dumb-founded. To be sure we would exchange butts through the week and the request was a normal one in those days. But after him throwing a full cigarette away ten minutes before! I asked him about it. His brow puckered up, surprised I didn't understand.

"Look, Healy - get this into your thick Charlestown skull: you have to keep the side up. You know who Micksie Murphy is in this town - they're the people we must impress. You never let the side down". I was not impressed by Micksie Murphy, his wealth, his directorship or his family or his rugby club presidency or whatever it was and I told Taxi so.

"You can shag off back down Bury Street and pick up that fag - and keep the butt for me".

"Lookit, you're missing the whole point of the exercise, Healy".

"I'm missing my butt - that's the point as far as I'm concerned: we haven't a smoke between us and we'll be here until two in the morning".

Taxi decided it was no use talking to me.

He wasn't without some experience in the matter. I wasn't a day in the office until he called me aside as we were leaving at finishing time. "Mister Healy, I would like to have a few words with you".

He wore his self-important face which completely took me in. We would go down to Johnnie Clarke's for coffee and cakes. I was very green.

Mister Hennigan wanted to know my starting salary. I told him it was a pound a week. He trusted I would keep that to myself. Journalists had a place to uphold in this town and if ever I was asked, I was to say I was on a salary of one thousand pounds a year.

"How much do you have?" I ventured.

"If anyone asks you what the chief reporter earns - that's me - you say he must be earning about two thousand pounds."

"But how much do you have?"

"Thirty bob a week."

And he dived into my packet of Players and helped himself to the third cigarette.

The thirty bob a week dropped the self-important mask from his face, and though he was to try and put it on again, as he came the heavy on the duties of a cub reporter towards his chief reporter he never quite succeeded in convincing me. I was now more of a conspirator in the game of keeping the side up and admission to the club was paid in sharing cigarettes or butts of cigarettes as the weeks went by. Still, as we were leaving he said, with a flourish,

"I'll allow you to pay for the coffees!"

Taxi had the gift of the grand manner. He was a member of the Rugby Club and played the game as well as writing about it. To be in the Rugby Club was to have arrived.

Taxi 's style was such that if social circumstances found him in the company of the town's top business men, he would step up to the bar and airily order six neat whiskeys, or whatever, and not worry that he was committing two weeks salary to the 'slate'.

Tony Burke, the third member of the staff, and himself had an evening ritual of two pints in Gus Doherty's pub on Bridge Street.

It was a favourite haunt for some crusty and very talkative English Colonial types, who came to fish salmon in the famous Ridge Pool on the Moy. Gus 'carried' Tony and Taxi on the slate for most of the week, chalking up the pints which would be paid for on pay-day. I was a non-drinker in those days - happily - but each evening went along for the company.

Irish pubs tend to be sepulchral places where conversation is carried on in small groups in an almost confessional way and since we had three rather pukka-wallah fishing types holding forth for three evenings in a row, at the top of their voices or so it seemed, this got on Taxi's nerves.

Taxi was determined to 'shut them up' once pay-day came. But on Thursday evening - with pay day still twenty-our hours away - it became too much for him.

Just as Gus was about to respond to fill a fresh round of drinks for the anglers, Taxi, with impeccable timing, called out loudly

"I say, my good man - let's have two large brandies - I have to do a broadcast for the B.B.C. in fifteen minutes time".

Gus, astonished at being "my-good-manned", dropped his jaw and the bottle and like a man transfixed, poured two brandies.

"Cheers, old chap" said Taxi , knocking it back.

Burke smiling, sipped his.

Gus, now looking dour, stood waiting for the money.

Taxi leaned over and whispered in his ear:

"Put it on the slate, Gus".

But the silence which had followed Taxi's imperious call also intimidated Gus, who might, another time, have exploded.

And folding his paper to tuck it under his arm, Taxi took his leave wearing his self important face, until he was at least half way across the bridge.

What with Taxi Hennigan rarely passing up a chance to keep the side up and Fred de Vere writing periodically in the paper that his was the highest circulating paper in the provinces and his staff the best paid men in provincial journalism, it was a rather hard act for a 'greesheen' from the village of Charlestown to follow, on a pound a week.

In truth, I didn't try - and yet looking back, we managed to knock out a fair good social life.

A year after I had started, the paper took on a new junior reporter from Ardnaree, a local lad called Michael Finlan. We were the one age and, as it was to turn out, had the same tastes in stories and music and humour. Mickey was a Gilbert and Sullivan buff and played the mouth organ and we lifted many a boring afternoon, he playing and I singing. Fred de Vere caught us at it a few times and tried to separate us but had no place in which to do so, having only the one small pokey office.

Although living at home, which included a public house and a grocery shop, Mickey was almost as hard-pressed for money as I was, but great boon, we managed the cigarette supplies.

We were mad Al Jolson fans to the point where we knew every note of every arrangement made for the re-make of Jolson's life in "The Jolson Story".

The way to riches, we decided, was to write one hit song and we'd have it made. Even then, in our teens, we were aware that many of the hit songs were stolen from classical composers and the big Donald Peers hit of 1949, "When You're in Love" was a souped-up version of "La Golindrina". Gilbert and Sullivan would soon be coming out of copyright - now if we could take a few of the well loved arias and re-work them in modern idiom, we'd have it made.

Finlan could play the piano and I'd write the lyrics - but who would we get to actually write the new music down in notes? No trouble, says Finlan, Paddy Sweeney, the band leader in Ardnaree

We actually got together with a piano and tried working

on: 'The Moon who's rays are all ablaze'. We tried it as a quick step, an up-tempo number like 'Throw a silver dollar', another hit that year, then as a slow waltz and finally as a foxtrot.

But since we'd have had to wait for a while for copyright to expire that project died.

We wanted money now - not fame later.

I salvaged a story out of it by sending to the *Sunday Dispatch* in London a piece saying Mayo bandleader Paddy Sweeney was looking for a song for Mayo, all entries to be examined, the winning one played and possibly recorded.

We didn't know what we were letting ourselves in for: within a week we had over one hundred songs from all parts of Ireland and they were to keep coming in for weeks afterwards. It would be almost a quarter of a century later that the town of Castlebar showed Finlan, Sweeney and myself what a good idea we missed out on when we hadn't started an annual song contest.

What Finlan and myself really salvaged was free dancing six nights of the week with Paddy Sweeney's band, for Paddy made us honorary band members.

Our job was to carry in the amplification and other gear and if the doorman wanted to charge us admission we merely had to say "We're with the band".

And so night after night we were on the dance floor as Sweeney struck up the signature tune, 'That's a-plenty', with brother Murdie sighing over "C'est ci bon" and our musical hero, Johnny Burke putting aside a fine jazz trumpet (and he was without equal in his day) to sing gravel-voiced 'Melancholy baby' or 'River, stay way from my door'.

We had the crack, good innocent fun. We had Gerry Sweeney, Paddy's youngest brother and a non-musician. He'd be as broke as we were and one night he had the problem of getting a drink without money.

He went into a huddle with Finlan who came out of it smiling, thumbs up.

Three minutes later Gerry collapsed on the middle of the dance floor, writhing in agony and tearing at his shirt collar. Everyone stepped away from him, making a ring around him. Finlan, in a half Groucho Marx lope (one of his favourite film characters) rushed across the floor, his ear down to Sweeney's feeble croak. He was just audible,

"Force brandy down my throat".

Finlan looked round the gaping crowd and, very much the man in charge, said,

"You heard the lad - force brandy down his throat".

Two or three showed signs of moving for the bar.

"Quick, man" said Finlan, galvanising them.

Two people arrived with brandies and Sweeney, genuinely half-choking on the stuff, was carried off the floor, allowing a knot of worried people to force brandy down his throat.

We would return to Ballina at two or three or more in the morning when I would slip quietly into Battle's home, there, never without fail, to find a quarter of an apple tart and a pint of milk waiting for me in the kitchen. No mother could be more indulgent than Mary Battle who treated me as family.

If I went home of a week-end and had left a shirt lying carelessly on the bed after me I would return to find it had been washed and ironed and left back quietly.

It was a comfortable and happy home and although we used to joke with Tommy in the office about having a cash register for a heart, in his home he was generous to me and so was Mary. She was, and remains, one of the best types of Christian women who believed in God and His Goodness and yet had a fine capacity for enjoying life. I thought many times in that house, that if I was lucky I would one day have a wife like Mary Battle.

In the end, in 1950, I was to leave it. I had seen Dublin three times and now we were All-Ireland champions and I had got a job as assistant editor of *The Gaelic Sportsman* at the fabulous sum of five pounds a week.

I had a small brown attaché case. It held one spare shirt and two pairs of socks. It was easy to carry.

There was one letter, my reference from Fred de Vere. In addition to saying I was sober, diligent and attentive to my work over the two years he was delighted to assure anyone concerned that "Mr Healy is also an excellent paragraphist".

The last sentence made me livid - nothing about my big scoops in the English papers! Nothing about my brilliant coverage of G.A.A. affairs and the biting commentaries which made the Mayo County Board sit up and back off when they threatened libel! Nothing but "an excellent paragraphist".

Well, poor Fred would be dead and gone and I would learn a lot, lot more about newspapers and newspapering before I would realise the fine tribute Fred had paid me.

I left Tommy and Mary Battle's home on a Saturday morning, lonely to be leaving them but elated that I had broken into Dublin journalism. I knew where I wanted to go in Dublin but I was keeping that to myself.

I had read all the debates in the Dail about the setting up of the Irish News Agency (I.N.A.). It would, said the Minister for External Affairs, Mr Sean MacBride, under whose Department it would operate, break the paper wall around Ireland and tell Ireland's story to the world: it would be staffed by the cream of Irish journalists. That was the phrase I liked: the cream of Irish journalists.

I would get four or five years experience in Dublin and then I would try and get into the Irish News Agency. It would take me that time at least, I thought.

I had five shillings left after I paid my single busfare to

Dublin. The landlady, I hoped, wouldn't look for her rent in advance.

As the bus sped on to Dublin I was all right for cigarettes for a while anyway. Mary and Tommy Battle had given me a present of a whole carton of Sweet Afton.

I broke the carton open at Mullingar to put it in my case. Inside Mary Battle had pinned a short note of Good luck and God Bless. It was attached to a five pound note.

Her husband might never get any nearer the Rugby Club than to photograph the Micksie Murphys for *Social and Personal* or *Tatler and Sketch*, nor Mary either - but she knew how to keep the side up for her own.

Michael Finlan

Mary and Tommy Battle   Photo: Mary Battle

SIX

My first job in Dublin was on the *Gaelic Sportsman*, a fortnightly G.A.A. paper. I had made my first contact with the paper six months earlier when I had sent it a story about Master Brennan, the local school-teacher in Curry, Co. Sligo who was blind and whose lifelong ambition was to see Sligo Senior Team back in Croke Park in the Fifties.

He devoted his life to this singular dream because his parish had supplied the backbone of the only Sligo Senior Team to grace Croke Park in the 1920s. The county had been cheated of supreme honours, but Master Brennan was sure that if his school produced a good juvenile team, it was the start of the road back. Year after year, through the Thirties and Forties his school salary went on footballs, jerseys and knicks for the Curry Team and now in the late Forties, even blindness would not let him lose sight of his dream.

With each new championship season, Master Brennan would be brought to the opening round when Sligo played, and led on to the field to meet the team.

When a new talent was added Master Brennan had to 'see' him with his hands, feeling the man's features so that he had a mental picture of him. Then he would sit sightless on the sideline while a neighbour 'broadcast' the match to him. And while Sligo would be beaten, as often as not in the opening round, Master Brennan would return to Curry to encourage his local youngsters yet again. It was a warm human interest

52

story which the *Gaelic Sportsman* printed prominently and the editor would be delighted to meet me if and when I was in town.

The year 1950 was the year Mayo won the All-Ireland Football Final. People talk about a national will and a national psychology and if someone had mentioned that to me on the last Monday of September 1950 I might have been puzzled by it. But there was no mistaking the elation at being a Mayoman who was only two hours away from the train home with the victorious Mayo team and the Sam Maguire Cup.

It is still a vivid memory for me, walking down the quays at The Ormonde Hotel, the setting sun warming again the old mellow bricks of this ancient city. It was no longer the cold, alien place I had first known in 1948 when Mayo came to Dublin to try for the All-Ireland honours, only to fail.

We had beaten the best and we had come from the snipegrass and we had taken on the best in the country and beaten them handsomely. We were the champions - the best in the whole of Ireland. And the more I looked at the city buildings the more confident I was that, one day soon, I too would come here and be the best in my business and it would be no trouble.

I felt it, in a most physical way: that sense of confidence was as deep in me that evening as the sun of the centuries in the red bricks I was looking at on the quays. We were the best in all of Ireland! And now, within six weeks, a lot more soberly, I was back in the city in this first job. My school pal, Stephen Doherty, was a bank clerk and in 'digs' in Grove Park, Rathmines, where he had got me fixed up. The job was on the north side of the city in Eccles Street. It never occurred to me then, or later, that I might take digs on the north side, and indeed I was to marry and set up home within the parish of Rathmines.

CHAPTER SIX

The *Gaelic Sportsman* was then being printed by the Fleet Printing Company. I was never sure of the hierarchical structure but Hugh McLoughlin and David Luke were there at that time and Hugh's future wife was secretary. It did job printing and published the *Farmer's Journal* and a few city magazines or monthlies.

Each publication had a cubicle-like office and if you were very tall you could look over the partition and into the *Farmer's Journal* or whatever.

The first day was a bit of a let-down. I had the title assistant editor but I found I was the staff - copy-boy, reporter, chief sub, make-up editor - the lot! The editor was Paddy Purcell and he was working for another firm. My first meeting with him was very informal and easy going. Later, when both of us worked for the *Irish Press*, I found it was his usual manner. There were no complications: I was my own boss. The contributors would send in their copy and laying the paper out was no problem. I agreed.

I am not going to say my heart sank when I discovered I had to produce the paper from scratch, also designing the lay-out which is a very technical job.

Firstly it calls for a knowledge of typography.

Now while Fred de Vere gave us all a great grounding in almost every aspect of newspapering he never let us near the stone, those benches where the galleys of type are gathered to become the pages of a newspaper, each story being placed in a pre-determined place by the stonemen who take their instructions from a lay-out 'dummy' under the supervising eye of a stone sub-editor.

The lay-out 'dummy' itself is a scaled down page of the paper on which the lay-out editor has sketched in his pictures and stories so that they balance as a composition.

In the *Western People* the chief engineer or his son made up the pages as they went along. They put in the columns of advertising first and then, depending on what material had been set, shovelled the copy in without any great regard for editorial emphasis. Lay out never changed from week to week very much and the only observance was to keep on regular pages. We were allowed to write our own headings or headlines and between headlines and sub-headlines we often gave the 'guts' of the story.

One staffman, whose brother was a solicitor in the county, used to have a field day when it came to court reporting. "BELMULLET SAGA OF HATCHET ATTACK IN PUB" would be the main headline, followed underneath with

"MY SKULL WAS CRACKED IN TWO HALVES -
PLAINTIFF"

and then

BALLINA'S SOLICITOR'S BRILLIANT DEFENCE"

and finally

"DEFENDANT GETS FOUR YEARS PENAL SERVITUDE"

And when we reminded our colleague there was nothing brilliant about a client getting four years he'd bounce back "If it wasn't for our Paddy he'd have got life". Yes

Anyway I returned to Eccles Street having seen the editor and decided I had better keep my mouth shut about knowing nothing about lay-out. The next edition was, mercifully, ten days away and somehow I'd work it out.

In my capacity as lay-out editor I should, ideally, be able to cast-off a story, that is, to be able to say how long a story would be in terms of metal, given that it was set in a certain font or size of type. Say, for instance, you had a seven hundred word story: an experienced sub-editor could tell you that it would make fourteen inches in a single column.

Now my neighbour in the *Farmer's Journal* was producing a paper the same size as the *Gaelic Sportsman*, and thanks to that low, dividing partition, plus a few, well-timed calls on him to borrow paste, a scissors or something else, I could watch how he was doing the job.

It was simplicity itself! All he did was to get his copy set after which he got galley pulls proofs of it. Instead of the miniature page, he took the actual full size page and pasted his proofs on to the page itself and then wrote his headline. whether it was to be a two or three column headline depended on how he pasted down the story.

Now the great thing about *The Gaelic Sportsman* was that the advertisements rarely changed from week to week so that there was no great variation on the shape of the pages. With a few back numbers of the paper and keeping an eye on my friend in the *Farmer's Journal*, I got stuck in and by the end of the week, if I couldn't cast-off a story to the last inch or so, I was able to master the rest of it like a reasonably competent lay-out man.

But I kept away from the stone because the men there were old craftsmen and would spot the greenhorn without any trouble. The men on the stone have a language of their own. It is the language of the printer. It is the world of measurements in ens and ems, picas, of stories set nut and nut, full out, on hanging indents, ragged right or left, upper and lower cases with types in bold face roman, san serif bold or italic and Gothic condensed. It is the world of half-tones and reversed blocks and type families which do not mix and in five minutes these men know whether you are a greesheen or a man who has learned his trade.

Yet as stone sub-editor and production manager in one, it was my place to be on the stone to give instructions if a story was overlong, so as to specify the cuts and, generally, to see so many pages a day were put together and ready for the machines. I stayed in my little cubicle and if the paste-down layout which I had done hadn't worked out because a late advertisement had to be accommodated, I let the printer come to me whereupon I merely knocked four inches off the story to allow him to accommodate the advertisement.

David Luke came to me one day and said I should not hesitate to go out to the stone to keep the printers on their toes. He took it for youthful shyness on my part. "Don't be afraid to boss them round" he said brightly.

My first edition was no great work of art and I didn't even bother to keep it. The next edition wasn't a great deal better and I doubt to this day whether anyone could tell where Healy started or finished in the *Gaelic Sportsman* barring he stumbled across a few signed articles which I wrote at the time.

I was to learn one thing very quickly, being full time on sport was no substitute for the excitement of hard news and, because I had in part anticipated this might be the case, I had deliberately held on to one stringership when I left Mayo. For the general rule was that you notified the daily papers or news organisation for which you were a stringer or corespondent that you were leaving, recommending a successor whose application was always in the same post as your letter of resignation.

The one to which I had held on was The Irish News Agency (I.N.A.). I had a hunch that, although I was now based in Dublin, it just might be possible to talk the news editor into leaving my name on the book as a stringer so that I could still have a foothold in the business of news. It never occurred to me to do the same with the *Times Pictorial* or the other papers: I accepted that they had Dublin offices and staffs and would have no need of a stringer. The same reasoning should have applied four fold to the I.N.A. but something - the guardian angel - said, no - keep that link.

I had re-worked some of my hardy annual stories for the Irish News Agency. Joyce Redman, the Old Vic actress, had taken over Bartra Island in the mouth of the Moy, in a home which an old recluse called Charles Kirkwood used to own.

CHAPTER SIX

She was expecting a baby and there was no phone link with the island and no other house or family. If she were 'short-taken' she had arranged to light fires on the shore so that a vigilant doctor would come by boat from the Killala or Enniscrone mainland.

I had got the stringership in the first place when the two top executives, J.P. Gallagher the General Manager and, the news editor, O'Dowd-Gallagher came to the *Western People* office to try and interest Fred de Vere in buying the agency service.

Fred was in a separate office by this time.

I wasn't ever sure whether Joe Gallagher, lighting his pipe, regarded me over the flame with an amused contempt for failing to recognise one of Fleet Street's hottest salesmen, but O'Dowd Gallagher was quicker off the mark. He saw a chance to pump a very willing young man for information which would allow him build up a better picture of Fred de Vere. He fired ten rapid questions and got ten equally rapid answers, and even J.P. listened with interest now. After I had dialled Fred to tell him they were in the office and would like to see him, Fred jovially told me to send them up. I went back and told them he'd see them and remember I said, he's going to tell you his is the greatest paper in the provinces, he is the greatest thing since sliced bread and unless you are giving a service for nothing he won't want to know.

The prediction was accurate enough. At least, a week later when I applied to be the I.N.A. stringer in Mayo I got the job and a lot of material telling me the kind of story the I.N.A. wanted.

It was a cold, clear frosty October evening when I climbed the warm stairs of 76-77 Grafton Street - Domas House - which was the first offices of the INA. Between the first Christmas lights I had seen and the glamour with which I had regarded the INA, employing as it did the cream of Irish

58

journalism, that stairs' climb was a tingling adventure.

It didn't matter if they wouldn't allow me to be a Dublin stringer - I had my valid excuse for entering the holy of holies even if I wasn't anywhere near the cream yet. To have gained admittance and to have seen the place would be enough and would sustain the dream for me.

A pleasant receptionist asked my business. I wanted to see the news editor, I was one of the Agency's country correspondents. O'Dowd Gallagher bade her to send me in.

I said I had come to tell him I could no longer cover Mayo for the Agency. He stopped me mid-sentence:

"Why not, old boy?"

"I have just moved to a job in Dublin."

He seemed astonished.

"But why didn't you tell us you were coming to Dublin?" The question threw me completely. Somehow he seemed to be annoyed and resentful - was it because I had left them without a man in Mayo?

Before I could say something he was on the house phone to the general manager telling him I was in the office, I had left Ballina and was now working in Dublin. It was staccato all the way and it had a curt ending. He turned back to me.

"Christ, old boy, we would have used you."

The sentence was hardly finished before J.P. Gallagher was bounding out of his office, hand outstretched in welcome and glad to meet me. I would have a drink - let's pop down to the Zodiac next door. Still dazed, I found myself flanked by both men in the Zodiac bar. I had a soft drink. Even now in retrospect the next few minutes are a jumble but the dialogue boiled down to one crucial, astonishing sentence:

"Would you consider joining the I.N.A. on a salary of one thousand pounds a year?"

No matter what I could say it was too stunning. Eight weeks ago I had just over two pounds and eleven shillings a week. Overnight that had become five pounds a week. Now a thousand pounds a year - to join the cream of Irish journalism after a mere six weeks in the Capital. It had to be a mistake. This simply couldn't be true or happening to me.

I was, I suppose, literally dumbfounded for once. It was, in their eagerness, mistaken for reluctance.

They had learned I was assistant editor of the *Gaelic Sportsman* but now looking back I was sure they had never heard of the paper and had mistakenly thought I had a very good salary there. It was O'Dowd who said, a bit testily:

"What do you say, old boy - one thousand a year and expenses, of course?"

I looked a him and said simply

"I am not worth a thousand a year - five hundred would be nearer the mark."

To my colleagues in the business that sounds untypical Healy for in the quarter of a century since then I've had my hard-nosed bargaining sessions which have resulted in the legend that "Healy never sells himself short".

And I truly believed at that moment on that night that my evaluation was the more correct one. I was a green country kid, barely up from Mayo and going in, as I thought, to be one of that great team which constituted the cream of Irish journalism.

Had O'Dowd Gallagher only known it, I'd have worked for my digs just to be in what I thought was an elite band. I think O'Dowd was surprised at my sentence but Joe Gallagher jumped in like a flash: "How soon can you join us?"

A week's notice was the traditional thing in those days but I said two weeks. O'Dowd shook my hand heartily and the General Manager added there would, of course, have to be an interview by the Board on Monday but he didn't foresee any difficulties. Would I be available at such a time? I said yes and we parted.

In my exuberance and elation I couldn't wait to write a letter to my bosom friend, Mickey Finlan. Instead I sent him a telegram (he was the only one to know of my ambition to one day get on the I.N.A. team) saying I'd been offered one thousand, repeat one thousand a year to join the INA.

A day later I regretted the rashness - what if I failed the interview? For three days I could barely concentrate on the job in Eccles Street. The nights were the worst. I lay awake in Grove Park, smoking cigarette after cigarette, trying to imagine what questions would come up at the interview, cold sweat breaking out as I fumbled question after imagined question. Had I made a mistake in saying I wasn't worth a thousand a year? Would that be interpreted as insecurity? And night passed into bleary morning and into questioning night again, and there was no one in this whole city to whom I could turn and talk, and the self assurance which was born on a September evening when to be a Mayo man was to be the greatest was now a very thin and insubstantial thing.

Finally the day and the hour came and I faced that Board. Conor Cruise O'Brien, thin lips pursed, Bob Brennan, former Irish Ambassador in Washington, glasses gold-rimmed but yet the severity of the face was softened by kindly eyes and Peadar O'Curry, editor of the *Catholic Standard*, shooting questions from the side of his mouth, a recognisable Bogart. A few general knowledge questions were fended with little enough trouble. What news magazines did I read? *Time* and *Newsweek*. What was the cover story in the current issue of *Time*? No trouble. And then, after a few more questions about American politics à la *Time*, Robert Brennan asked me if I would venture a guess as to *Time's* political slant - did it favour the Democrats or the Republicans? That, I figured, was the key question - and I didn't have an answer.

Truth to tell I was more interested then in the snappy style of the writing than I was in spotting the slant. It never occurred to me it might have a slant. To me, newspapers and magazines of substance were free of such things as biased reporting or party slants. I answered I didn't really know. That was the last question and the end of the interview.

Two mornings later I had a formal letter in the post offering me a job as reporter at an agreed salary of three hundred and fifty pounds a year plus expenses. I sent another telegram to Finlan in Ballina to confirm I was on the staff.

The following week Fred de Vere, taking the story from the two telegrams to Mickey Finlan, proudly front-paged the news that a former *Western People* staff reporter had joined the Irish News Agency at the excellent salary of one thousand pounds a year. The figure was in the headline.

The kudos for Fred and the *Western People* was that I was a prodigy of Fred's training and like so many distinguished journalists who had received their basic training under him I was now, in less than two months, joining - you guessed it - "the cream of Irish journalism".

I had some misgivings about he headline and the figure and rang Finlan to explain. Mickey said: "Arrah what the hell, three-eights - that's what they offered you, wasn't it? Leave it at that - you're keeping the side up, kid".

And so I left Fleet Printing, Hugh McLoughlin and David Luke for Domas House and the cream of Irish journalism, supremely happy to be working at less than half of what they thought I was worth. Within three months I knew I had made only one mistake. I had sold myself short by fifty per cent.

It was the first time and the last time I ever did that...

John Healy and Michael Finlan - 1951

SEVEN

It seems incredible now, looking back from the vantage point of the 1980s, that Ireland counted for so little.

True, we had got self-government for the twenty-six Counties less than thirty years before. We had stood aside in World War Two and now, with the great post-war reconstruction of Europe taking shape, Ireland's role and voice was not to be seen or heard.

The days when Mr. de Valera was head of the League of Nations had gone up in the battle flames of Europe and our last European link - Sean Lester as High Commissioner of Danzig - was lately back in Ireland, having been a virtual prisoner of Hitler in Switzerland for the war years. The United Nations was still a young idea and indeed it would fall to the new Coalition Government of 1948 to lead Ireland out of isolation and back into the mainstream of world politics. It would also declare the Twenty Six counties a Republic in, as Prime Minister John Costello said, fondly but wrongly, the hope that the action would "take the gun out of Irish politics forever".

The big domestic political issue from the Treaty onwards was Partition. Every political party, excepting the Irish Labour Party, operating on the island as a whole, owed its existence to the division of Ireland. In the South, Sinn Fein had split after the Treaty to produce what came to be known in our day as Fine Gael, the United Ireland Party and later

Fianna Fáil, the Republican Party.

Recurring bouts of para-militarism against the Unionist North of Ireland had, like republican rhetoric from South of the Border, done nothing more than entrench Unionist politicians and Governments all the more firmly on Stormont Hill. For most of that first free generation in the South we did little else but snarl at the Unionists of the North with their "puppet Government" and their armed police state as represented by the Royal Ulster Constabulary and the "notorious B Specials", a para-military auxiliary police service manned in the main by Protestants. The Unionist Party had a built-in majority from the outset and ensured its continuance by a system of gerrymandering constituencies and by discriminating in employment against the substantial Catholic minority. The Nationalist Party which represented the Catholic minority took the Dublin Republican line that the Northern Parliament was a puppet one, doomed to failure, and they did not at first participate in the parliamentary political process.

Britain, in point of fact, was creating a political slum in that part of Ireland she held to be part of the United Kingdom. Although there was direct representation at Westminister and Northern politicians were seated there, the convention was that the House of Commons did not discuss the affairs of Northern Ireland. The Stormont Parliament, on the other hand, accepted and passed into law measures adopted by the House of Commons. You had, for instance, in these first post-war years the anomaly of a socialist Westminster government under Clement Atlee, passing socialist policies which a conservative Unionist administration in Stormont simply had to accept and implement. Implementing socialist policy on a doubly conservative North was, however, much more preferable than living and working with the "priest-ridden, Rome-dominated Republicans" of the

CHAPTER SEVEN

Free State in the South.

In the South, Eamon de Valera came to power in 1932 with his twin national aims of abolishing the evil of Partition and restoring the Irish language. He had sixteen years in office on the trot and had Ireland in the palm of his hand, yet the twin aims seemed to be harder than ever to resolve. There had been bouts of militarism by the I.R.A. and, though proscribed, the movement continued underground at varying strengths.

De Valera, the constitutionalist in power, was to imprison or detain and indeed execute some of the more extreme republicans who threatened the internal security of the Republic. Some republican elements, dissatisfied with the lack of progress in abolishing Partition, gathered around Sean MacBride, former Chief of Staff of the I.R.A., to launch a new party, Clann na Poblachta, the Children of the Republic and it contested its first general Election in 1948 with Fine Gael and Labour as well as the Clann na Talmhan Party, a small farmers' party started in Mayo and stongest in Mayo, Galway and Roscommon.

Looking back now we were to witness for the first time, but not the last, that curious Irish electoral phenomenon of the way the Irish people use proportional representation to discipline and renew the nation's most effective political machine, the Fianna Fáil Party.

The Irish, being an agricultural society are by nature and culture conservative. Each small-holder of five acres is a capitalist. Thus there has never been a polarisation of politics on the Left-Right model, despite intensive campaigns by the Labour Party and such distinguished men as Dr. Conor Cruise O'Brien to create a Left-Right confrontation.

For much of the Republic the alternative to a Fianna Fáil deputy was a Fine Gael deputy. Both were equally conservative, both believed in a United Ireland, both opposed

66

the Partition of the country but the Fianna Fáil man had the edge because Eamon de Valera was the great verbaliser and leader, the last surviving Commandant of 1916. Politics in Ireland had polarised on the issue of the Treaty. Fine Gael had been the pro-Treaty Party, Fianna Fail the anti-Treaty Party. The issue had produced the Civil War and bitterness, and it was the fuel of domestic politics and just as passionate as the extremes of capitalism and socialism in its intensity.

You have to keep pinching yourself in these days of the 1980s, when you have a directory full of vocational and professional organisations, to remember that in the 1930s and 1940s so complete was the polarisation of our republican political society, if not of society itself, that the only local organised units in any town or village in rural Ireland were the Fine Gael club or the Fianna Fáil cumann.

The major farm organisations of today's world were decades in the future. There were co-operatives of a kind to run creameries but even those were politically dominated.

It was a stratified society which even the Gaelic Athletic Association, Ireland's largest voluntary sports organisation, did not cut across: the more Republican the G.A.A. became the more it closed out Fine Gael pro-Treaty followers.

Culturally the moral tone of the nation was set by the Bishops who, each Lent, published mini-encyclicals inveighing against late night dancing, gambling, sexual impurities and the evils of communism in a country which wouldn't recognise a communist even when he was labelled as such.

In such a society you do not look for political mobility and in the Ireland of the Forties, Mr. de Valera had every right to expect that, given the numbers, he would be returned to power in 1948.

When you have had sixteen years to build up a Christ/anti-Christ value system you can feel reasonably certain that, while some of your own followers may be a bit disappointed at the lack of political achievement, and their original loyalty might be waning because of, say, the treatment of one-time fellow republicans, they will not desert to the anti-Christ of the party, the pro-treaty crowd called Fine Gael and popularly known as the Blueshirts.

Mr. De Valera was, as always, right.

Except that in Sean MacBride's republican-hued Clann na Poblachta and the middle of the road farmers' party, Clann na Talmhan, dissident Fianna Fáil supporters had a choice between Christ and anti-Christ, and took it.

They could, and did, vote for Clann na Poblachta and Clann na Talmhan without feeling they were letting down the anti-treaty side. The result was as much an electoral shock as the post-war defeat of Winston Churchill. New men were in office and among them was the former I.R.A. Chief-of-Staff, Sean McBride who was to become Minister for External Affairs, the man who would end isolationism and bring Ireland's story to the world, including the growing, festering wound of Partition and the manifest injustices under which the gerrymandered Catholic minority had to live in the North.

MacBride's preoccupation with the world-wide dissemination of news was to remain a consuming and abiding interest with him for thirty long years after he had left office, and as a Nobel and Lenin Peace Prize winner he would use his international reputation to seek to improve international relations and world peace by preaching the gospel of better news' dissemination.

In 1948, the republican gun laid aside, as de Valera had laid it aside, he would not only see that Ireland's story was told to the world by Irish newsmen and feature writers, he would also bring to the world's attention the plight of the Catholic minority in the North under the Unionist regime.

Mr. de Valera's Fianna Fáil Party opposed the legislation creating the Irish News Agency. The mood was such that the Party would have opposed the Ten Commandments had they been introduced by a Coalitionist Moses and, indeed, later we would hear a future Minister of State declare that the I.N.A. was nothing but "a bunch of Reds". In that bitter election campaign of 1948 Sean MacBride was to speak in Ballaghadereen and his voice carried to St Nathy's College where I was a student.

I was to say the next day in class that he had made a good speech only to have the priest-teacher jump down my throat. Mr. MacBride was a communist - and since the cap fitted he could wear it and anyone else who thought like him. It was as near as I ever got to a civics' lesson in that establishment.

Yet the Red tag was to remain, like many other things, a factor in the history of the Agency. There were others of a more serious nature.

The first was the tag "government sponsored".

A free press in the Western world looks with suspicion on government sponsored or controlled news gathering services. They regard the output of such services as little better than propaganda. Other nations in Europe created their own national news services but the attitude of non-national papers to them remain pretty suspicious.

The Press Association and the American Associated Press are news cooperatives, financed by weekly, daily and week-end or evening papers. This financing guarantees their independence of a government subsidy and therefore, it is argued, government interference.

Ideally a news agency formed on a co-operative basis by Irish publishing houses would have been far more effective but at that time in the 1940s this concept was outside the ken of Dublin managements. It still is: they have their own profitable problems today.

There was a second problem. Many of the 'stringers' for the British or American papers saw in the Irish News Agency a threat to their earnings and for this reason refused to supply services to the Agency and were hostile to the idea. The stage was reached indeed where Irish news, meaning news originating within the Republic and sent to the I.N.A. in Dublin, could not be circulated to the few daily papers which took the I.N.A. service. The ironic exception to this was that news from "the sundered North" could be circulated by the I.N.A. as being non-Irish! Partition and the Border has produced many a weird turn in Irish life and the I.N.A. was not to escape it.

A sample story shows the absurdity of that restrictive agreement. Say a newsman in the I.N.A. had got an exclusive story that Aer Lingus was to buy three Jumbo jets from a U.S. firm. You couldn't circulate that story under a Dublin dateline to the Dublin papers. But by the device of slapping a "Belfast -Thursday" dateline on it and quoting that the I.N.A.'s Northern editor, Paddy Scott "had learned reliably in Belfast late tonight" that the order had been placed, the agency could then circulate the story internally in Ireland.

The big fear of the Dublin journalists was that the I.N.A. would become something like the Press Association, covering the courts and the Dail and Senate to which the separate papers then had to send teams of four or five men each day.

An I.N.A. team of, say, three men each in the Dublin courts and at the Oireachtas would, by delivering a verbatim service to the morning and evening Dublin, Cork and Belfast papers, have effected a great financial saving for the papers concerned. The restriction on circulating Irish news internally effectively put an end to that.

It lost the I.N.A. a very good source of revenue, forcing it back on Government funds to a greater degree and thus reinforcing the tag that it was little more than a propaganda service.

The Irish market was small enough but the early management team led by the general manager, Mr. Joseph Gallagher, who was vastly familiar with Fleet Street and its hustling methods, was somewhat lacking in sensitivity on the more pedestrian and very stolidly conservative Irish scene. It was to become part of the legend of the I.N.A. that when he tried to sell the *Irish Independent* group a news service and encountered some benign opposition he is said to have promised, in finest Fleet Street fashion, to make the *Independent* sorry for the decision.

The *Independent* in 1948/1949 was the most successful publishing house in the country and their powerful daily morning paper could still afford to put nothing but small ads on Page One with the death notices. No Reverend Mother, parish priest or curate was dead until they died in the *Irish Independent*. It was the era in which distinguished visitors were taken to the roof to be photographed and the odd one might enquire, on being shown through the great works, where was the little man who sprinkled Holy Water on the papers before they were sent speeding to the four corners of Ireland for the benefit and edification of that paragon of virtue "Catholic Mother of Twelve" who, after after the bishops and Archbishops, set the moral tone of the country.

Joe Gallagher, Fleet Street hot-shot, would have been somewhat out of his depth in the sanctum of Mr. Geary who was responsible only to the Murphy's (then owners of the *Irish Independent*) and God in that order! Later, when the I.N.A. issued a picture of tanks rumbling by in a Moscow May Day procession, letting it out with a translation of the Russian caption as it came in on the wire picture, the Irish Independent used it to attack the I.N.A. as a purveyor of atheistic communism. The Art Editor who thus got tarred

71

CHAPTER SEVEN

with the "Red" tag is none other than Kevin O'Kelly, who went on to become religious correspondent of R.T.É. and he was no more a communist than any of us in the outfit at the time.

I knew little or nothing of these problems the first morning I started work at the Irish News Agency.

To me it was enough that I had, overnight as it were, joined the cream of Irish journalists. I was raw enough but O'Dowd Gallagher the news editor, an expansive Irish South-African, ex-war correspondent had clearly taken a liking to me and took time to explain news agency practice to me. There was also a former Reuter's war correspondent, Jack Smyth of Galway, a dapper, red-headed reporter with a slight American accent from his days in Japan and Berlin.

O'Dowd gave me the elements of a first class story. Remember the four C's - get them all into one story and you have a page one story: Crime, Cash, Cunt and Cookery. Smyth, used to writing for the A.F.N. newscasts, had the second great lesson "Kid, tell them you're going to tell them: tell them: tell them you told them". Anyone who has ever listened to an American radio bulletin will recognise the wisdom of that. You repeat the key central point of the item three times, operating on the theory that the first mention of, say, an air crash will merely catch their attention on the word "crash". So you repeat the word "crash" in the second sentence and add that ten are feared drowned. Your third sentence says "hopes of survivors from the crashed plane which had a crew of five and five passengers are fading". Matthew, Mark, Luke and John, the four best PRO's in the world had the same idea, and simplified their ideas just as effectively.

I was to be given some training preparatory to becoming the I.N.A.'s first district staffman outside Dublin. I was, in fact, to be posted to Shannon Airport, 'the crossroads of the

72

world', as we called it in those days.

It sounded very romantic and very exciting - and just a little overpowering for a young man of twenty-one who was fresh from doing the Charlestown notes and news and would soon find himself in the cosmopolitan world of Shannon Airport where he was supposed to identify, on sight, the newsmakers of the world from film stars to European Prime Ministers going to and from Rome, Paris or London, to New York or wherever. That would also include our Minister for External Affairs, Mr. Sean MacBride who would, I felt sure, be watching critically how one of his agency's young men acquitted himself in the task of bringing Ireland's story to the attention of the world. In the meantime there were a few less lofty things to be done and when a British heiress, a slight blonde, took off for Ireland with her boyfriend the hunt was so intense that Fleet Street forgot about the propaganda tag and turned to the I.N.A. in the hope that it might just come up with something - preferably a photograph of the couple, old boy. Exclusively.

I was to deliver that after a chase on a punctured bicycle!

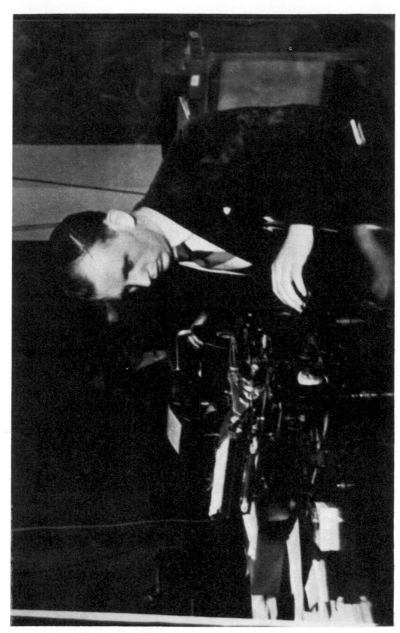

John Healy at his typewriter in the Irish News Agency.

EIGHT

Bringing Ireland's story to the world through the medium of news was easier said than done. Through news and photo-features, yes, but on news alone it was a hard sell. The All-Ireland Football Final or Hurling Final might be the biggest news story in Ireland for two September Sundays but the world didn't want to know how the games went.

But you could get a bit of space for a news-feature article on Micheal O'Hehir, the boy broadcasting wonder whose story, as an overnight success, was great copy. A new quote, giving his forecast for the big game, gave you a chance to re-work the same basic story each year: all you did was change the relevant figures of how many All-Ireland broadcasts he had under his belt and you could tell the story again of how, as a mere kid of seventeen, he had talked the national broadcasting company into giving him a chance to do a running commentary on the big football games.

A story like this which you can write year after year at appointed times is called 'a hardy annual'. It was the hardy annuals which became the bread and butter of the Irish News Agency in the first four years of its existence.

The British Sunday papers were then fighting for marginal circulation in Ireland and, while these had their own staffmen and stringers, the columns of the Irish editions were to be a fruitful field for the I.N.A.

The same British papers still regarded the I.N.A. with

suspicion: it remained suspect as a Government financed agency. That merely upped the challenge to the staff and the trick was to dig out stories and write them so tight and punchy and - very important - with so good a headline on them that an antagonistic news editor or chief sub-editor would be forced to use them. These stories were sometimes hardy annuals. They ran to about five hundred words in length and always ended with a good punch-line - a sentence which left you smiling or sad.

We called these 'Sundayers' because of their popularity with the Irish editions of the British Sunday papers.

The trick was to get a good headline.

A prime example of the 'Sundayer Hardy Annual' was the old Wexford habit of catching eels on the mudflats. It was a traditional method of walking on ski-like timbers to spear the eels. Each year when the season opened we wrote that story with the same headline:

"THEY'LL CATCH EELS - ON SKIS!"

I was back to my *Times Pictorial/Sunday Dispatch* days in Mayo, catching rabbits (dash) with a Gramophone (exclaimer). Always the exclaimer!

Now writing Sundayers was right up my alley because I had served my time very well in the hungry grass of Mayo where sheer necessity had sharpened the wits to look for the angle which would give you the headline and the inevitable exclaimer. Very soon, as part of my training, I found myself teamed up with Jack Smyth as the Sundayer team.

It was formula writing at its best and worst and if we ever tired of it (and we didn't) there was always the Sunday morning excitement of getting over a dozen English Sunday papers, counting the 'score' and, more particularly, studying the stories to see if our English counterparts were able to improve on our headlines. In most cases they didn't or couldn't. In those days we assumed they couldn't. Once I became familiar with newspaper production methods and editionising for various regions I began to have second thoughts: if a story is reasonably bright and well headlined you merely process it and get the page away, rather than waste time in fiddling around with different headlines and such like.

Breaking into the British dailies was another problem. Most had staffmen here. If, by chance, we had a good story running and the local staffmen missed it, the call back to their Dublin offices brought the response: "It's from the I.N.A.? That's the Government propaganda outfit..."

One great causes celèbres in those days was "The Battle of Baltinglass".

Baltinglass is a small village in Wicklow. Miss Cooke, the local postmistress, had been left the post office by her aunt whom she had assisted for many years. At that time in Ireland the allocation of a post office was a major political and financial plum and when Miss Cooke's aunt announced her intention of retiring the village expected that her niece would succeed her. After all she had served for years with her aunt and had no other means of livelihood.

The Coalition Government of the day, figuring it was Buggins' turn, decided however to advertise the vacancy. Even then the village expected it was a formality and that Miss Cooke would retain the post office and be confirmed as postmistress. To the consternation of the village, and later the nation, the job went to Mr Michael Farrell, a young, well-to-do shopkeeper at the other end of the street.

Political favouritism, shouted Fianna Fail, as if that party in its sixteen years in office ever did anything else but give such plums to loyal party followers. (Indeed in my own hometown several years before we had the same situation over a post office - except this time Fianna Fáil was in power and gave the plum to a local party member who had a public house. The difference was that the Fine Gael opposition of the day did not back the Clann na Talmhan man, fiery Dominic Cafferky, when he tried to 'expose' it in Dáil Éireann. Besides, the Opposition did not have a daily paper like the *Irish Press* to personalise the story.) At any rate the issue became a first class human interest story and between the *Irish Press* souping it up, Fianna Fáil in Parliament charging corruption and favouritism and portraying the slight, silver-haired lady, fighting a great State bureaucratic machine, it became a big international story with newsmen flying in from Europe.

The alliances formed were disparate to say the least. We had the official Republicans of Fianna Fail, the patriots who abhorred all things English and British, starting with the Royal family, aligned with Queen Elizabeth II's cousin, who left her pigs to join the protesting picket line, along with some local British Army Desert Rats men, to support Miss Cooke.

Michael Farrell and friends ran a brilliant campaign and telephone engineers sent to remove the cables to the Farrell premises ran into trouble of all sorts.

I was sent to Baltinglass and told by O'Dowd Gallagher: "See if you can get Farrell to speak - he's the story if you can get an interview with him".

Miss Cooke talked freely. Mr Farrell wouldn't give me or anyone else the time of day. I filed my stories, morning and evening, faithfully calling on both sides for the latest developments. But Mr Farrell was adamant: on no account would he talk. Morning and evening it was "no comment" and his silence was now the big story.

The longer he remained silent the more desirable became an exclusive interview. O'Dowd kept hounding me. In desperation I started to look for some common ground I might have with him which would give me an opening: it seemed a thin prospect. I told him about our own post office crux a few years before but he seemed to regard it with suspicion. Then I heard he was a member of the F.C.A. or Local Defense Forces. So was I.

It was to prove the opening I needed. After the usual "no comment" one morning I inquired if he had been on basic training with the Army. It was something to talk about other than the row and we talked about square-bashing, firing a Lee Enfield .303 for the first time and the bad barracks food.

We had shared experiences, it seemed. By the second morning when we had exchanged more army training experiences, I remarked, with what I hoped was a certain amount of diffidence, that as someone who had soldiered in an Irish uniform I found it ironic that a ranking officer in the British Army Desert Rats should be taking the other side in the village and be praised for it, and that a man who thought it worthwhile to wear an Irish uniform should be portrayed nationally and internationally as the villian of the piece.

It struck a chord: if I came back that evening he'd give me his side of the story.

So he did. That night he gave me the facts about his life and why he had applied for the job as post-master and indeed the sacrifice he had to make for wearing an Irish uniform, something which had displeased a grandfather of his to his detriment.

It was late when I finished. The story would make the London evening papers and many others and would be repeated in the morning papers. He promised he would not talk to anyone else. I phoned my exclusive story and within the hour all hell had broken loose in the journalistic corps in Baltinglass as British office after British office called back their staffmen saying they'd got an exclusive interview with Farrell from the I.N.A.

Michael Farrell was as good as his word: he had said all he

was going to say and he had no further comment. Naturally disappointed the staffmen had to call back that he was refusing to talk to them. He would only talk to the man from the Government sponsored I.N.A., the Government mouthpiece and obviously it was a set-up job by the Government. Months later, with Fianna Fáil back in office when an opposition deputy retrieved a copy of the interview from an American paper and tabled a series of questions in the House, the Fianna Fáil Minister was able to assure him that barring one small unimportant detail, the interview was totally accurate and fair in all respects.

The Battle of Baltinglass, we were to say later, helped undermine confidence in the first Coalition Government and led to its downfall in 1951. It wasn't as simple as that. The Irish electorate had sent Fianna Fáil into opposition to reshape itself and had taught it a lesson: it was prepared to forgive Mr de Valera and send him back, chastened, to office.

The Protestant minority in the South, others would say, would never forgive the Taoiseach, John A. Costello for breaking a link with Britain by declaring the Republic. Others still would hold Dr. Noel Browne of Clann na Poblachta responsible, saying he was intransigent in the face of the opposition of the Archbishop of Dublin to his Mother and Child scheme. And any time an Irish News Agency staff-man beat the staffmen of the British papers on a story in Ireland they sang the old refrain: "That's Government propaganda - you can't trust that outfit".

In truth there wasn't much we could do about it - except to go on beating them if and when we could. There has to be a limit to everything and even the most hard-necked competitor can't put down a runaway British heiress and her lover as "Irish Government propaganda". At that stage you realise there are professionals on the job and you reach for the cheque book so you can have it exclusively, old boy.

The story is worth recalling now, if only because it demonstrates the uphill fight the I.N.A. had in some sections of the British Press. Lord Beaverbrook's Express group regarded the I.N.A. with disdain. It could afford to with its good crackerjack Irish staff. And the betting was that it would be the *Daily Express* which would track down Baron Liverpool's daughter, Pamela, who had run away to Ireland with her boy friend to be secretly married.

They didn't talk about cheque-book journalism in those days but it was just beginning. O'Dowd Gallagher, a former Daily Express staffer, got a tip that the lovers had rented a hire-drive car from Shelbourne Motors in Dublin and would be returning it in a day or two. We had separate pictures of the couple which O'Dowd had me study before posting me to keep the garage under observation. If and when they arrived in the Ford Popular I was to call the office. He gave me the car number. As I remember it now it was something like ZJ 322.

O'Dowd had that great habit of making every story he marked you for sound like the biggest story on earth. "Find them, old boy, and we'll blow Fleet Street wide open".

For four, long, miserable days I shadowed that garage, standing in the open and, hopefully, inconspicuous enough. Every car which came and went, irrespective of make, was checked. But the lovers never showed. On the fifth day O'Dowd pulled me off the story: the trail had gone cold.

By now, of course, on or off duty, I had developed the habit of checking every number plate of every car I passed, or which passed me, and if that now sounds like an impossible task you need to remember that the bicycle was the popular transport of that day and cars were not as numerous as today.

I had a bicycle myself on which I cycled to work in Grafton Street and one evening, shortly after my fruitless shadowing of the Shelbourne Garage, I was leaving the office at six when Jack Smyth asked me to have a drink in the

CHAPTER EIGHT

Zodiac Bar. I had a date with the girl who would become my wife, but I had time for one drink. It was the first time Smyth had asked me and I was flattered for I was an avid listener to his experiences as a war correspondent. He also clearly liked the facility with which I wrote Sundayers and since we were more and more responsible for handling the Sundayer service, we had a bond pairing of a kind which overcame the age differential.

An hour later we left the Zodiac and I had retrieved my bicycle. The back wheel was flat and I was cursing my bad luck. I was facing up Grafton Street and saying goodbye to Smyth when a Ford Popular came down the street with three other cars. The number was wrong but there was no mistaking the blonde beside the rather scraggy looking driver. The cars had passed me but I shouted to Smyth

"It's them - the runaway lovers". I jumped on the punctured bicycle and, coat belt trailing behind me, pedalled frantically after the car, hoping Smyth had heard me or understood. Bumpety-bump, bumpety-bump I went, praying that bloody car wouldn't go too fast and I could keep up with it! It turned round into Suffolk Street and I had it still in sight. Now I was panting with excitement. It turned into Trinity Street and I re-doubled my pedalling. As I rounded the corner into Trinity Street myself, I found the car parked outside the now demolished Moira Hotel. Parking the bicycle I checked the hotel from the doorway. I was just in time to see them walk into a corner table in the dining room. There was no doubt now - they were the runaway lovers alright!

O'Dowd's instructions were clear: don't scare them, just call the office.

Would I risk taking my eyes off them? What happened if they decided to leave while I was phoning. I hailed down a taxi and gave him a pound:

"Get in behind that Ford there and if it drives away with a

couple in it follow it at all costs.

"Here" I gave him O'Dowd's card with the I.N.A. number on it.

"When it stops call this number and ask for this man. Whatever the fare is will be paid".

The taxi-man was a bit non-plussed by this cops and robbers stuff but he was reassured by the pound note: you got a lot of taxi miles for a pound in those days anyway.

I got through to O'Dowd. Symth had got part of the message I had shouted but didn't know what had happened once I'd taken off: all they could do was sit and wait to see if I called in. Within four minutes O'Dowd, to my great relief, was on the scene. I pointed to them at the corner table. Like a pointer he was rigid with as much excitement as I was.

"Leave it to me, old boy. And thanks. Great work. Go back to the office and wait."

O'Dowd discharged the taxi with another pound and I wheeled my lame bicycle back to the office to wait.

Within an hour O'Dowd was back in Grafton Street with the lovers. They were photographed a dozen times from a dozen different angles. Joe Gallagher was in; Features' Editor Rushworth Fogg was in; Smyth hadn't gone home. Now the major offices in Fleet Street, London were being called by the senior men. "I.N.A. here, we have the runaway lovers. We are offering exclusive Dublin pictures and story: what are you prepared to pay? Thank you we'll call you back."

The *Daily Express* topped the bidding, especially when O'Dowd explained that the I.N.A. had just signed an contract with the couple for the exclusive, marriage pictures and exclusive, honeymoon story. That was one night when Fleet Street never mentioned Government propaganda service!

The runaway lovers were low on funds and O'Dowd had done a deal for the exclusive wedding and honeymoon pictures. The I.N.A. detailed Smyth to get the lovers off to a hide-away in Wicklow with a photographer. So we had a running story each day, with pictures, until the registry office, early-morning marriage.

I limped home that night with my bicycle and an apology to my date. After I told her the story, she was as excited as I was. It was just as well. She would have many a night in the future when the job came first and she came second and, mercifully and thankfully, was always understanding about it. If newspapermen are born and not made then the same goes for the best newspapermen's wives.

John and Evelyn Healy - 1952

NINE

A news agency, to compete successfully, must first have the requisite technology. Basic to this is a teleprinter link into each major publishing house. This would mean a teleprinter in the three, Dublin morning papers, in the *Cork Examiner* and the *Evening Mail* as well as, in Belfast, the *Irish News*, the *Northern Whig*, the *Belfast News Letter* and the evening *Belfast Telegraph*. In the London context we would have required twice that amount of machines.

In fact we had one teleprinter line from the I.N.A. head office in Dublin to London and all copy transmitted to and from London had to be taken by a typist, stencilled and corrected and then sent round to the various offices by messenger. We were just about marginally faster than Reuter's original pigeon-post, one hundred years before.

Yet it says something for the calibre of men like O'Dowd Gallagher and Jack Smyth that they were so imbued with the challenge and could so imbue people like me, that we actually lived and worked to the motto: "Be first, be fast, be accurate". We phoned and wrote our copy as if we were a real news agency where seconds counted in getting a story on the teleprinter.

In the Press Association, Associated Press or United Press when a story breaks there is a well-practiced tradition. Remember that when one man sitting at one machine in Dublin or London starts to tap out a story, it is going into every news organisation with a teleprinter link. Viewers of sporting programmes will now be familiar with the teleprinter chattering out the football half-time, or full-time scores as they come into the television sports desk. At the same time the same results are stuttered into evening newspapers all over these islands as well as to the Sunday newspapers.

What the television viewer doesn't see is that in the newsroom, as distinct from the sports section, there will be a bank of teleprinters carrying the services of the differing and competing agencies whether Reuter, U.P.A. or A.P. or A.F.P., the official French news agency. It is on this bank of teleprinters that reputations are won and lost in seconds. The greater bulk of the day's news is transmitted as a matter of routine. But when the unexpected happens, like a sudden disaster, an airplane crash or the collapse and death of a leading figure, the normal copy flow is interrupted, a bell is activated and the cryptic first bulletin called a 'flash' is sent out e.g. "De Valera dead".

The offices are now on full alert. The second message may be a 'snap' sentence which reads more fully: "President Eamon de Valera of the Irish Republic died today, aged ninety". Once the story is started and, hopefully, yours is the first agency in with the news, you have scored on the counts of being first, being fast and being accurate. Sustain that kind of operation and you win contracts and earn revenue.

Now there we were in those days of the Fifties going through this second-by-second drill, sending out flashes and snaps to London as if the London office was somehow electronically linked with all of Fleet Street when in point of hard fact, we knew the London office's speed of delivery was governed by the availability of a typist to make a master copy which had to be duplicated, after which you hoped the messenger boy of the day wasn't snarled up in some London traffic-jam or hadn't ducked into Mooney's for a fast pint! One other method on a really big story was to deploy whoever was in the London office to phone the more important papers with the flash. This still had to go through a switch and a copy-taker before it reached the news desk - by which time the competing teleprinters of the other services were in full stride.

In truth then, the I.N.A. couldn't even begin to compete, lacking as it did the basic technology of a news agency. Yet a critical Dáil Éireann and a hostile, Dublin Press corps insisted on treating it as a full-blown commercial agency and, from time to time, questions would be tabled as to the progress it was or was not making.

The standard question, and the critical one, was concerned with the question of contracts secured abroad. Some of the questions came from a Fine Gael deputy whose brother had been made Dublin manager of an American news agency and, I fear, the interest was not always declared or made very obvious.

In the event, the first British contract to be made was with the big, Odhams Press Group. It happened when the provincial news editor of the weekly *Melody Maker*, Jerry Dawson, rang and asked if the agency could let him have a service from Ireland, reporting the activities and movements of musicians and band leaders. O'Dowd Gallagher was racing ahead on the sound of the magic word "contract" and assured Dawson he had the right staffmen to cover the musical beat - when did he want first copy? We would file (or send) copy to London or Manchester. Did he want it by phone, cable or printer? First post on Tuesday morning would do said Dawson.

"Fine, old boy - first copy will be with you promptest on Tuesday."

Now O'Dowd hadn't a clue what the *Melody Maker* was all about and like me, had never even seen a copy. We looked up a Press Guide and found it was one of Odhams rich stable of trade periodicals; specialist weekly papers or magazines which ranged from mass circulating, womens' weeklies to sober, technical journals like *Kinematograph Weekly* .

The excitement in the office couldn't have been greater had we just signed an exclusive contract with *The Times* of London. I didn't quite understand it at the time, but it enabled the management to be able to report progress with the securing of a contract - the magic word - with the Odhams Group, one of Britain's giant publishing houses.

That would, and it did, set the Dáil Éireann knockers of the I.N.A. back on their heels. No matter that it was only for a couple of guineas a week, with extra for pictures: it was a contract and with a readily identifiable, British publishing house. You didn't press the matter with supplementary questions for fear they gave the Minister an opportunity to expand on the success.

We purchased a copy of the *Melody Maker* and O'Dowd detailed me as the agency's musical expert: I would be responsible for fulfilling this vital contract.

He was a great man to brief a junior reporter. Suddenly, if I did 'a bang up job' on this contract, it would open the whole of the Odhams Press to the I.N.A. This was the break we'd been working for, 'old man'. And now it was up to me to expand the small bridgehead we had achieved. Deliver the goods on this contract and he'd talk other editors in Odhams Press into accepting contracts for regular coverage out of Ireland. It was all up to me.

Fortunately the assignment was right up my alley as one who, at that time, spent five out of seven nights a week dancing in the Dublin ballrooms. I knew all the bands and most of the band leaders on sight, and when they heard I was covering Ireland for the *Melody Maker* they were only too glad to co-operate with news of the movement of personnel, what contracts they were signing and with whom, for the summer or winter seasons.

It was also the time when the big British bands like Joe Loss, Ted Heath, Victor Sylvester, Oscar Rabin and many others were beginning to find an Irish tour a very profitable one. In the 1950s dancing was about our biggest industry in rural Ireland and two or three promoters had cornered the traffic in bringing in British bands who could cream off three hundred a night playing a big ballroom from nine to three a.m. The competition led to the formation of the Irish Federation of Musicians who would later stipulate that a relief Irish band had to be employed, thus protecting the available work for their members.

This was a repeat of what the Americans had done ten years before when the growth of the record industry and canned music threatened the live musicians 'livelihood'. James C. Petrillo struck the recording studios, pulling out the big bands from behind singers like Sinatra, Ella FitzGerald and others, a strike which gave birth to harmony group, backing singers with lush orchestra-like sounds. The Americans limited tours by British big bands and Britain retaliated.

For a decade this transatlantic, cold-war went on preventing British musicians and fans from hearing the best live performances, by new, big names like Stan Kenton. Jerry Dawson and his editor at the *Melody Maker*, Pat Brand, had little time for such restrictive ordinances and between them they found a way to let their readers hear Stan Kenton and Woody Herman live in Europe. Dublin was the key. The Irish Federation of Musicians' under General Secretary Paddy Malone, had no quarrel with Petrillo because the Irish Big bands playing Vegas were something in the future.

Kenton could play in Dublin. The *Melody Maker* arranged for the hiring of the old Theatre Royal which could then seat three thousand and organised a sea-lift for fans with a one-day, round trip to Dublin, just to hear Kenton's orchestra in the flesh.

In fact over four thousand made the trip to the astonishment of the Dublin newspapers to whom the whole idea seemed weird, not understanding the long years of Anglo-American union hassles.

Dawson was delighted with the I.N.A. service and now, having looked up Willings Press Guide, we hit on the idea of trying to break into the trade periodical field. Shortly afterwards we got a second contract from another technical publication in the Odhams stable and I was detailed to service that too.

We had no opposition here, no local Irish correspondent to compete with and because, generally, the firms which advertised in these technical journals sold their goods in Ireland too, news of Irish contracts was welcome. More important, advance news of contracts about to be awarded alerted advertisers to a potential market, making their subscription to the magazines doubly valuable.

In the first years the Agency closed down at midnight and did not re-open until eight-thirty in the morning. Later when Douglas Gageby became editor-in-chief, we remained open all night. The spell of duty from midnight to eight in the morning was known in the business as 'the lobster trick'. We tried it as an experiment as much as anything else and it had a success of a kind.

London had more evening papers then and evening papers always suffer from a copy famine in the first three hours of the day. When the best part of half your world was asleep, the agency men on the lobster trick could do little more than re-write and 'top up' or freshen stories which had already appeared in the morning papers.

Land news copy on an evening editor's desk at seven or eight in the morning, when he has yawning pages to fill and linotype machines demanding copy, and he doesn't much care where it comes from so long as it reads and is printable. Similarly a news editor, who has an editor barking for copy of any kind, isn't going to worry about government sponsored propaganda news, so long as it helps fill the early pages. He can junk the stuff later and replace it with running news as the world comes to life and cars have accidents and courts hand down sentences and film stars arrive in on morning flights from America or wherever.

I was still technically a junior reporter when I took on 'the lobster trick'. Being, by nature, a night owl, it suited me vastly. The drill was simple enough. You got the early editions of the Irish morning papers round midnight. I learned to divide the night into 'traders', that is, stories for the trade magazines and, when the city editions came in at three-thirty or so, 'eveningers' or stories specifically aimed at the London evening papers for the first editions.

There is one word which has no place in news agency vocabulary and that's 'yesterday'. Yesterday is history.

When, at four in the morning, you cannot ring someone up and inquire as to the up-to-the-minute position, you soon learn the art of the 'throw forward' story to up-date it and make it current again. A man who had been eaten by a lion in the morning papers might be a dead story in Dublin, but with a throw-forward introduction it could read: "Dublin police are expected to order an inquest today into the death of lion-tamer John Doe, whose pet lion broke loose and savaged him. In the meantime, his thirty-six-year old, blonde wife, mother of three, is recovering in a Dublin hospital this morning."

The London, evening social diaries were another market we singled out and The Starman's Diary in the *Evening Star* was a favourite of ours. O'Dowd Gallagher had been on the *Daily Express* and had knocked around Fleet Street for many years before coming to Dublin. He was on first name terms with men like Arthur Christiansen, the editor of the *Daily Express* and he could ring them up offering exclusive items or stories if and when he thought he could do a better deal for the agency in that way. The operation was primarily aimed at goodwill-building. The evening paper diaries were always a soft mark during Horse Show Week, when the young British deb-set descended on Dublin's leading hotels for a week of high jinks. The resident, titled members of the peerage were also surefire copy for the *Star* or the *Standard*. Thus when Lady Oranmore and Brown, a scion of the Guinness family, decided to hold a twenty-first Birthday party for her son, Gay Kindersley in Luggala House in the heart of the Wicklow mountains, the London diarists, who had been refused invitations, came on to the I.N.A. to see if we could cover the going-ons for them. As usual O'Dowd promised them it was no trouble we'd have a man there.

They could depend on the good old I.N.A.

Gay Kindersley had been the subject of a bitter, court action for custody after the marriage of his mother broke up. He was the centre of the London 'smart set' which, for this party, would transfer the action to Wicklow.

Luggala House is set in a valley at the bottom of some of Wicklow's most rugged mountain terrain. Access was by a single road, a glorified goat-track, which could take but one car at a time. For the party strict security precautions were easily enforcable. A check-point Charlie on the top of the mountain path stopped all traffic from proceeding down the road to the house in the valley. At the bottom of the path was a second check to scrutinise the arrivals and pass them through to a magnificent car-park among the trees of the lawn. Anyone contemplating the gate-crashing business, without trying this route, had to be prepared to be a Sherpa Tenzing.

As usual when O'Dowd Gallagher made expensive

commitments, Healy, the office bright spark, was going to be the go-for once again and by now I was beginning to catch on to his pep-talk bit about opening up Fleet Street or, in this case, the whole London Diaries' scene. "Bring off this one, old boy, and we've got it made with the diary editors". I wanted to believe it, of course, and did. We knew the local staffmen had tried to get an invitation and failed. To get in and get a good eye-witness account of the festivities would help counter their notions of a propagandist service.

By a stroke of luck one of our directors was an invited guest. O'Dowd had arranged that if I failed to get past the security, this man would meet me at midnight on that bleak mountain top and slip me as many names as he could remember.

I arrived in Roundwood, the nearest village to Luggala House, at dusk. It seemed a prudent thing to scout the territory first and no better place than in a village pub where, hopefully, some of the locals would have some gossip which might be a help.

I made a less than credible figure in that local pub, sipping a lemonade. Everyone knew a real newspaperman was fond of a drop of the hard stuff. It may be that I was so obvious that one or two of the locals smiled patronisingly on me and assured me I was wasting my time trying to get in. Then I learned about the check points.

Well if all went to all there would still be my midnight informant.

The bar-keeper said there was a lot of coming and goings all day, and 'Herself' (Lady Oranmore and Browne) had laid on a great spread altogether with a firm of caterers out from Dublin and there was nothing but vans coming and going all day with eatables and drinkables - "enough to victual an Army" - was how he put it. Now this in itself was good copy - the kind of local colour story which the English evening papers liked.

Slowly it occured to me, that if there was so much coming and going of catering people, I might just get past 'check-point Charlie' by posing as an assistant catering manager sent out to check on last minute details.

I had a big, American, chauffeur-driven Dodge and if it only succeeded in emphasising my youthful skinny figure, well then I was only a young assistant. We drove up to the check point and the driver, who was a few years older than me, let down his window, gave the name of the catering firm, a fictitious name for his assistant manager and we were nodded through, the message being relayed ahead of us to the check point at the bottom of the valley.

We repeated the scene at the second check point and drove by with the assurance of tired professionals.

Once on the grounds proper we pulled the big car in under the trees in front of the house and lay 'doggo'. I had a good vantage point. In the main drawing room the curtains had not been fully pulled. A fire blazed. Two figures stood in front of it. One was Lady Oranmore and Browne. The second was the unmistakable figure of Erskine Childers T.D., then a widower..

On the lawn to the right of the house two huge marquees had been erected. One was for serving food and drink, the second was for the dancing. The band leader was the current darling of British society, Tommy Kinsman.

The guests were arriving fairly quickly now but they were all strangers to me. One or two Dublin personalities were among them and they were identifiable enough though hardly Star Diary material. I was logging the tunes Tommy Kinsman was playing when, suddenly, someone appeared at the car door. Politely but very firmly I was asked to come to the house. In the hallway I was met by Her Ladyship's Secretary. She was short and brusque: "You, Mister Healy of the Irish

News Agency, are an intruder. You will quit the grounds - or do I have to call the police?"

Behind her, grinning was Dublin society photographer, Charles Fennell, known to a few of us affectionately as 'Slippy Tit' Fennell. Charlie didn't like anybody, much less the I.N.A., poaching on what he rightly regarded as his exclusive territory, the Big-House scene and he wasn't exactly broken-hearted to see me off the premises, I think.

There was no point in making a scene so I left. It was after ten and I would only have two hours to wait for my midnight friend. He was very punctual. I had occupied my time drafting my story and had merely to add the list of English debs and their titled escorts when he arrived on that windy mountain top.

We did clean up the next evening in the London diaries but it didn't blast the diary scene wide open and it brought the I.N.A. no great fat contracts. Ebullient O'Dowd was delighted, of course. While the coup might have chipped another bit off the suspicion that the I.N.A. was basically a government propaganda service the fact remained that no one wanted to talk contracts and, more sadly still, there was all too little evidence that the Irish News Agency was achieving the task of breaking the paper wall with which Britain had surrounded us.

True, Desmond Fisher in the London office had a good friendship with Tom Hickey, then editor of the *Statist*, and Des could and did place some 'heavy' pieces on the Irish economy in *The Economist*. Our Feature Section under Rushworth Fogg at first, and later novelist, Philip Rooney, that most gentle of men, who never had the temperament for agency hustling, achieved limited successes in far flung magazines in Australia and Germany. If we sold a feature series - Famous Irish Ghost Stories or Great Irish Murder Mysteries - to some of the British Sunday papers it was merely for their Irish editions.

The Paper Wall remained more or less intact, despite the efforts of a dedicated team of professionals.

John Healy and Michael Finlan make music with staff from the Irish News Agency.

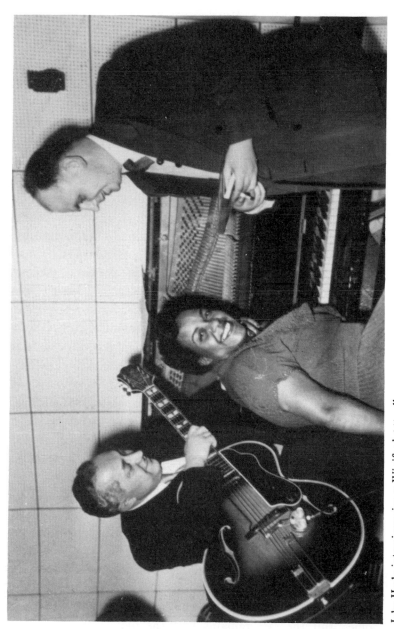

John Healy interviews singer Winifred Attwell.

TEN

Was the I.N.A. then a waste of public funds, a noble experiment which ended ignobly? Not quite. The metropolitan press, excepting the *Irish Times*, gave it little encouragement but the provincial press gave it a marginally better hearing. There it could supply a service which was relevant. Thus a reporting team in Lourdes for the annual, diocesan pilgrimages provided the Agency with copy, which local weekly papers took as well as with a plastic photo-block service which was a great boon then to provincial papers.

Many provincial papers had no women reporters in those days and when the Agency circulated them with a sample Women's Page column, several of them contracted to take it. The I.N.A. didn't have any female reporters at that time so I became Joan Duffy, Woman Features' Writer, yes!

But if we couldn't penetrate the hostile, British Press what about America? There could be no question of a transatlantic, teleprinter link and a New York office on the London model. Our service to America, for the most part, was by airmail and it went mostly to the Irish-American papers which were little more than saloon ad-sheets, scissors and paste jobs with news pirated from Irish provincial papers.

This may sound harsh coming from an Irish professional and may even antagonise faithful readers for whom these tatty New York produced weeklies represented a link of a kind with home. But the fact remains that the glory days when such weeklies were vehicles for the Fenian movement with plenty of muscular writing had long gone. They were happy to get anti-partition copy and use it, and indeed if one were to judge the I.N.A. mailer service on what appeared in those papers, it would force one - wrongly - to the conclusion that it was indeed a government propaganda service.

To be sure the feature section did topical news features on the situation in the North and the gerrymandering which existed in Derry in particular. But the news section covered the daily news out of the North including Stormont sittings and political news stories.

Paddy Scott was our Northern editor and there wasn't a politician, Unionist or Nationalist, Paddy Scott didn't know and couldn't ring at any time of day or night. Scott had more stories in him than any ten men in Belfast. The problem, as the head office in Dublin learned quickly, was to get him to sit down at a typewriter and write the bloody things. Scott would say he wasn't an agency man when, in truth, he was the very reverse. Dublin could ring Scott with a query and he'd listen and say: "Aye, I understand you. Listen now and take this down."

In ten minutes you had a column of a story, accurate in all its detail and informative. But to get him to sit down and write it - no, that wasn't Scott's way. A few notes on the back of an envelope and give him a phone and that was it: he'd dictate it without any trouble.

The English Sundays used to run an "Eire" edition for the Republic and a Northern Irish edition for Belfast and there was an opening for a Sundayer service if only we could get Scott to write it.

Years of reporting for the *Irish Press* had fixed Paddy Scott in his habits and his copy tended to have a lot of comment in it, which suited the *Irish Press* down to the ground. Today he would have been an ideal Northern Political Editor because of his long and vast experience covering the Stormont political scene. However - as in the case of Brendan Malin, the former *Irish Press* political correspondent who joined the Irish News Agency, writing agency copy which had to steer dead clear of editorialising was a difficult task at first.

They were, like the editor-in-chief Dan O'Connell, men of a different generation to mine, great shorthand note-takers who could read them back with pinpoint accuracy. They had come up in the school of reporting accurately what a man said, putting most of it in indirect speech and occasionally quoting directly the more critical passages. It was not an easy matter for them to change overnight to the five hundred word sprint when they had been marathon twenty-six mile men by training.

An example makes the point best. The old hands were used to this sort of an introduction:

"Ireland would never be at ease and would not prosper as a nation until the evil of Partition was removed by Britain who imposed it" was stated by the Taoiseach, Mr de Valera, when he spoke in Leinster House on a motion condemning the partitioning of Ireland by Britain, and he said that we would never rest until we had secured the freedom of the Six Counties".

The New School, to which Smyth, O'Dowd Gallagher and myself belonged as Agency men, would re-phrase it thus:

"Ireland would never prosper until Britain abolished Partition." So declared sixty-five-years-old Irish Premier Eamon de Valera in the national parliament tonight. And, he added, Ireland would never be at ease so long as the Border between the Republic and Northern Ireland remained. Mr de Valera told the House, "Ireland has an inalienable right to national unity."

And so on. Mind you, trying to get one short succinct de Valera sentence could be difficult, for the man was so careful in his qualifications that old time note-takers might have a de Valera quote making a full page of a notebook - and still be without a verb!

It says something for the democratic nature of the staff and the good relationship and sense of camaraderie which we had developed that no umbrage was taken when the old hands turned out stories and O'Dowd Gallagher, would hand them to Smyth or myself, and tell us to rewrite them, making them punchier. Which meant nothing more than a short, tight introduction, a tight second sentence followed by a quote which substantiated the claims in the first two sentences.

Paddy Scott was an old hand - and to say that is to mislead one straightaway for Scott, still active today in Ulster Television, remains as enthusiastic as any starry-eyed cub reporter in his zest for a news story.

Ostensibly I was sent to Belfast to beef up the coverage and help Paddy as the office 'go-for': privately my riding instructions were to get hold of Scott for an hour or two every day, sit him down, and shake the stories out of him.

Paddy was old enough to be my father in age, yet he was young enough to be a colleague. I did relieve him of troublesome, office chores and when he'd come back from Stormont I'd sit him down for ten minutes while he gave me a resumé of the debate.

"O.K. Paddy - I'll type it for you and phone it"

"Aye. Great. All right. Now - take this down"

But I had already my lead sentence and the second one. I'd read it.

"Aye that's fine"

"All right - now what's the actual quote?"

And Paddy had it, to a 'T'. In an hour we'd have three or four stories out of the day's debates, nice, crisp copy.

Very soon Paddy got into the habit of dictating the stories as tight as I'd have written them, for though he protested he

CHAPTER TEN

was an old dog who couldn't learn new tricks, he had them all in a month. But damn me if he'd sit down to a typewriter - it still had to be the scribbled notes and the copy dictated on the phone.

I enjoyed working in Belfast.

The Press corps had no fear of the I.N.A. and there was none of the resentful surliness one found, too often, in Dublin. And even though reporters were nominally broken up into Catholic and Protestant there was a camaraderie there in the early Fifties which I still remember with great warmth. They had a healthy cynicism and if it didn't always surface in their papers it wasn't their fault. They did a straight reporting job and if the chief-sub or the editors of the day pencilled it out in aid of party politics well then you shrugged your shoulders, had another pint and said "another day, another dollar".

The I.N.A. service out of Belfast was as wide ranging as two men working fairly hard could make it. Edmund Warnock, Q.C. was a one-man opposition to the Bookeborough Government. He had been denied advancement by the landed gentry of Stormont and he was continually threatening to expose Unionism. He never did - but he provided good copy. When Brookeborough attacked the South we carried it fully and impartially and if it had to be backgrounded, we did it by attributing it, in a follow-on story, to Northern editor Patrick Scott, clearly labelling it as comment.

My first election in the North was for the seat of the Rev. MacManaway who was debarred from taking his place because, as a clergyman, he had held an office of profit under the Crown. Jack Beattie was selected to run on the Labour ticket against the Unionist candidate. It was a tough, working-class constituency which was later held by Gerry Fitt, and it was going to be touch and go. Jack had his final

104

rally in the Falls. Paddy covered it while I covered the Unionist rally in Sandy Row.

The place was a riot of Union Jacks and bands. From a second storey window over a local pub a loud speaker blared tribal speeches about Lundys and traitors. I sailed in and up the stairs to identify the speaker only to find that it was Willie Hamilton, an executive of a charitable organisation on whom I had done a few Sunday paper stories. He seemed a little taken a-back but I waved to him cheerily and carried on.

It didn't matter a damn to me - a man's politics was his own entitlement: my job was merely to report him accurately. Jack Beattie won narrowly and I recall that election now for two reasons. In the Beattie camp were two young men involved for the first time in the age old Belfast game of electioneering for an old stager. Their names? Gerry Fitt and Oliver Napier. They served their apprenticeship in a hard school.

The winning majority was thin enough for Jack Beattie to lift his hat in passing Milltown cemetery where, once again they rested in peace, their names having done duty well enough, to give Beattie the seat.

The second thing I recall is making sure the I.N.A. was first into Fleet Street with the result of the by-election in time for the Dublin and Manchester editions of the morning papers. The count was in City Hall. It had only one public coin-box phone. By agreement Scott went to the count while I manned the phone and kept an open line to Dublin. All we needed was the flash: "Beattie elected". It would make the late news boxes. The results and actual figures could come later. Scott, a veteran of such counts, came out on the balcony and shouted down to me at the foyer phone: "It's Beattie". I called it down the line to Dublin, pressed down the buttons and then quietly opened the mouthpiece and removed the diaphragm, screwing the mouthpiece back and replacing the phone in its

105

cradle. I was already in another phone-box outside the City Hall when the rat race started for the foyer phone. The Press Association man had lost the race to the foyer phone, and there was much banging of buttons and shouts of "operator" from the man in possession as Scott passed him on his way to the phone outside City Hall where, with an open line, he gave the final figures to Dublin and had finished before the milling reporters inside remembered that public coin box outside City Hall.

When I explained the mechanics of the thing to him the following morning he laughed.

"Another of O'Dowd's tricks, no doubt" he said.

No doubt at all! Be first, be fast, be accurate - and if there's only one phone and it develops a fault after you've finished with it, so much the better!

Belfast was a marvellous experience for a young twenty-one-year-old from the Mayo snipegrass and a town where a Protestant was someone who was late for Last Mass or didn't bother at all. We didn't have Protestants in Charlestown and I was a tender seventeen before I met a real live Church of Ireland family in Collooney while staying with Aunt Millie Phillips in Tubberbride. They were the Mahon family, good farming stock, where I went each evening for the milk. The house had one daughter, Ena, who would be about twenty then, a beauty in the Botticelli manner, a winsome lass in every way and a naturally open girl.

Aunt Millie would quiz me on who I met at the house, and when I replied the old people and Ena, she asked me what I thought of Ena. A very nice girl, I replied, very straight forwardly.

Now Aunt Millie could curse like a trooper and if she wanted to warn you off someone there'd be a string of epithets wound round the person's name. But the Mahons were very good neighbours and genuinely nice people.

For once Millie found it awkward.

"Ena" she said, "is not one of ours"

"What do you mean - she's not one of ours?"

"She digs with the other foot."

"What are you talking about Auntie Millie?"

"She's not a Catholic" she got it out finally.

It was my turn to be non-plussed. All I said was "Well?"

She said nothing more but I knew what she wanted to say: "Don't go smelling round there".

I still remember that if I thought I had a chance of 'getting off my mark' with Ena Mahon, Aunt Millie's unsubtle strictures wouldn't have stopped me but when you are seventeen and in that mawkish period when you are just out of adolescence you don't have the guts to bone a good-looking woman for a date. And maybe the theory of the mirror-image does work. Meet someone with an open honesty of mind and you get it reflected back. At any rate I had gone to Belfast with an open mind, determined to do a good job and completely unconscious that it would be any different from Dublin. I didn't see Catholics or Protestants or Presbyterians - just Belfast people. What Willie Hamilton made out of me when, after I had surprised him at the Sandy Row microphone, I'll never know. He seemed a bit edgy until I told him it was a great night - and so it was for a greesheen from the Mayo snipegrass who really had no interest in the tribal battles of the Falls and the Shankill other than to report them even-handedly. When you've grown up with Bolshies and Blueshirts, Papes and Prods aren't that much different at election time!

What I did enjoy no end was a Belfast Sunday morning. After going to Mass from Cicero Gardens in Castlereagh I'd spend the rest of the morning going round the lay preachers who flourished at many street corners or on the steps of the Custom House. They fascinated me. We had nothing like them at home or even in Dublin, barring the odd man or two who might appear at Abbey Street corner from time to time of a Sunday evening when you had a big game in Croke Park.

Every man had his own bag of snakes whether it was drink, fallen women or gambling and he let it all hang out for the greater glory of the Lord God who reached down and picked him up and saved him personally. You stood with the little knot and listened and if I said anything at all to myself it was "Ah sure God love him - he's doing his best".

And so they were.

I don't think they harmed anyone, or corrupted anyone. They enriched the texture of life in that industrial city which had its own share of ugliness and its very real sense of evil was twenty years in the future.

I was to go to The Field on the Twelfth and the day after see the mock battle of Scarva where the Croppies always had to lie down at the end of the day. The Bolshies and Blueshirts again, ritualised now and not unlike The Mummers of Wexford with their uniforms and tap sticks and verses, re-enacting an older tradition of the morality play. The Pattern field at Tample outside Charlestown where after we had Christianised a pagan well with a decade of the Rosary, we repaired to the local meadow for an inter-village tug-o-war or a seven-aside football game when we were not racing or jumping, wasn't a million cultural miles from The Field.

A quarter of a century later I would meet little 'gets' from the North and elsewhere who escaped to Dublin to winkle their way into my business and who would count it a good day, and themselves good Republicans, when they purveyed the green side of the story and sold their orange neighbours short. Yes - and had the audacity to tell you "you people from the South don't know what it's like to live up there". Which is one reason why I will always have the height of respect for the old hands like Paddy Scott or Jimmy Kelly of the *Irish*

Independent: they were reporters first and commentators after.

It can be said today that I was very naive indeed. We are all so smart today in what we say and write about the North that I wonder we weren't all rich long ago. You didn't have to be very smart, sitting in Stormont thirty years ago, to see that it was indeed a puppet parliament, a Protestant Parliament for a Protestant people. The reality of the armed Royal Ulster Constabulary was very real indeed to someone reared with an unarmed Garda Siochana. The B Specials, "the dreaded B Specials" of the propaganda tracts, were real enough too.

But the plain people of Belfast, in their day to day lives, did not give a tinker's damn about the debates on Stormont Hill or who said what, anymore than the plain people of Dublin paid undue attention to the politicians of Leinster House with their sterile, Civil War bickering. And if Sandy Row put on a show for The Twelfth, strung bunting across the street and banners proclaiming "God Bless Our Queen" before marching to The Field to hear the Reverend Mr Smyth make a sermon which was vastly familiar, were they much different than the parishioners in City Quay in Dublin where Moss Street would be strung out with the same bunting for Corpus Christi, windows would drape the Papal Flag and banners invoke God's blessing on "Our Pope" as the children sang hymns through the streets?

Look at it how you will, it still comes out as the Numbers Game. And whether the manipulators are priests, rectors or politicians, North or South, it is the plain people of this island who catch it in the neck or the back when the game hots up and the rhetoric breeds bombs and bullets.

The very language by which we live becomes corrupted, debased and defiled and if nice guys finish last then surely the bastards must finish first.

John Healy, Irish News Agency, Belfast.

Patrick Scott, Irish News Agency, Belfast.

ELEVEN

Bill Redmond was on duty that morning.

The Editor wants to see you". The Editor was Douglas Gageby. The paper was the new *Evening Press*. Most people in the newsroom of the *Irish Press* thought him a detached, aloof and therefore cold person. I was writing a novel at the time and used to bat out a chapter a night. In the lull when the first country edition had gone, he would ask to read the latest piece of "the epic", to encourage me.

This morning he was in no such mood.

"You heard the morning news" he said.

A baby had been kidnapped. The only clue - and the only picture - was held by a house-to-house photographer who took the child's picture just hours before she was kidnapped.

He looked through the glasses, very evenly and spoke very slowly until there was almost a menacing note; "You will go out and you will come back with that picture."

There was no choice. The odds were truly enormous. No one knew the street photographer's name or where he had his headquarters. As well, the Garda Police Commissioner announced that one thousand five hundred Gardaí were on the case, searching for the photographer. A police announcement had been broadcast on the national radio asking him to come forward.

Then there were the Fleet Street papers. The *Daily Express* man had a cheque for five hundred pounds. The *Daily*

Mail was equally keen to bid for the picture exclusively.

On top of that there was the location. Ballyfermot then was a lot less developed than it is today; it was a sprawling shapeless mess of Corporation houses, rushed up to solve a chronic housing crisis in the capital. One road looked like the next: one avenue like another.

A very real fear filtered through the streets of Dublin. Four years before, a baby daughter, the child of street news-vendors, Mr. and Mrs. Browne, had been snatched and despite an intensive search had never been found. It was for this reason that every available policeman had been assigned to the hunt for the street photographer.

The enormity of the task sank in with little trouble.

I would need all the luck I could get and all the help I could muster. There were two people I was sure were in Heaven: one was my father and one was my first girlfriend, Maureen Cambell of Swinford. I literally prayed for 'the break'. It was not the first time and it would not be the last . . .

The Ashmore household that morning was a bedlam of newsmen, photographers and neighbours. No, there had been no news of the baby. No, they hadn't heard from the photographer and the young mothers crowded round the distraught mother, comforting her, "the 'babby' would be alright."

I got the description of the photographer. He was of medium height, stocky build. He had a red check lumberjacket, the neighbours assured me. You couldn't mistake him if you saw him, they claimed. If he turned up with this mob of newsmen around the place he'd be trampled to death. There was no way I was going to stay to get knocked down in the rush.

The Ashmores lived in a sort of inner park and when you emerged from it you had a choice of directions you could take. At the junction all I could say was "God direct me" and chance it.

Cliff Bedell the staff photographer with the *Daily Express*, had followed me. I had hoped he would take the opposite direction. He stayed with me. We walked some ten, pretty aimless minutes. Twice two police cars passed us.

We rounded yet another corner and there, large as life, was a stockily built man, hair-line receding, a camera hung on his bulging waistline which strained the buttons of the red check lumberjacket.

"That's him" I said and ran to catch him before he turned into a garden path with his batch of picture-proofs. Bedell, lumbered with a big speed-graphic camera case, came running after me. With something of the fierceness with which Gageby had charged me, I hissed in the ear of the photographer: "You're on a fiver if you give me the negative". He looked at me in total disbelief. "Remember" I said as Bedell panted up to us.

The man didn't know what I was talking about but the promise of a fiver was enough. Now he was all ears. I explained we were looking for a picture of Pauline Ashmore which he had taken yesterday afternoon,. He took hundreds he said: he didn't know their names. He never took names. Just pictures. He went back the day after and if the mothers liked the picture he took the name then.

Alright, we'd go back and get the Ashmore family to identify the baby.

By the time we reached the Ashmore's, the press corps had disappeared. The neighbours crowded round the photographer who showed them proof copies.

"That's Pauline," said one.

"No it's not - that's the O'Brien girl".

This was no use: we'd have to trouble Mrs Ashmore herself. The photographer dealt through his bunch of proofs like a pack of playing cards. One came up: "That's my baby" said Mrs. Ashmore, breaking down completely.

"Alright ma'am. We are going to put it in the papers and someone will know her. The birthmark on her forehead will show up and you'll have her back in no time."

She wanted to hold the picture, naturally. I turned to Bedell for back-up support: "Isn't that the best thing - to get publicity." Bedell, who had a strong British accent, didn't make speeches, but agreed.

I gentled the photographer away. Now Bedell was running a little ahead of me. It gave me time to whisper to the photographer that he was on a fiver so long as I had the negative exclusively.

His "studio" was in a private house in Walkinstown. We got a taxi. He would have to hunt up the negative. I said we'd wait. It was now coming up to eleven and the country edition had to be off the stone at twelve-thirty that afternoon. He had a partner who was a great deal slimmer and sharper and they very obviously held a conference in the hallway. The photographer came in and assured us he'd find the negative as quickly as possible. Then I heard the front door banging closed. Bedell and myself had to wait. I told Bedell it was getting close to edition time so if he didn't mind, we'd go to the *Evening Press* first and we could give him a copy of the picture, chat-chat-chat.

The hall door opens and the sharp one returns to announce that he has just rung an evening newspaper and has been offered a tenner for the negative. I jump in to say we could double that but he would have to come to our office first. Bedell started to enter some reservations and I headed him off:

"Look Cliff, let's not argue - we don't want to lose it to someone else".

"They are on their way to collect it" said The Sharp Man to underscore the urgency.

A tenner was almost a week's wages then and I didn't own a cheque book.

"Come to our office and you get twenty quid".

He was less than sure.

"I tell you what: let our photographer friend here come with us. You stay here and meet your client: if your pal here doesn't get twenty pounds he calls you and he returns with the picture which you can then sell."

He agreed. It would be twenty minutes to the office and he'd have his call before midday.

We arrived at the back door of Burgh Quay and I pounded up the backstairs through the machine room.

Gageby came charging through the caseroom door against me, his face in a very rare rage. "Where the Christ were you - we've had the picture stolen from under our nose!"

No, you haven't" I said. "Here's the photographer and the negative for twenty pounds".

Those who know Douglas know he is not overly given to public emotion. He just said "Good man" and threw his arms around my neck, then grabbed the photographer and left Bedell and myself standing.

Bedell started to growl. I told him he'd be alright: he'd get a print later...

I sat down to write the story. Later I learned what had happened. The Sharp Man, like the photographer, an Englishman, came out to try his luck at raising the ante and not knowing the Dublin scene, saw a big display poster advertising the new *Evening Press* and rang it, offering the picture for a tenner. We were bidding against ourselves - but then I was afraid of my life to ring the office in case Bedell got inside me. Jim Downey was dispatched by taxi to Walkinstown to collect the negative only to find the birds had flown. Crestfallen, he called in to say some other paper had got the picture and that accounted for Gageby's rare rage.

In the excitement Gageby had said nothing about my missing the country edition with the picture and story. The news at one-thirty led with the missing baby story and repeated the appeal to the street photographer to come forward with the picture which police now described as "a vital clue" in their hunt for the kidnapper.

The first city edition of the *Evening Press* came up. I was dumb-founded. There was no story or picture. The other evenings, the *Mail* and *Herald* led on the story with the *Herald* banner headlining the story:

"UNKNOWN STREET PHOTOGRAPHER HOLDS VITAL
CLUE TO KIDNAP"

We brought our main evening edition forward with a big splash story and filling most of the top half with Pauline Ashmore's photo. The quote was from the mother:

"THAT'S MY BABY"

It was a good old-fashioned scoop.

Then all hell broke loose. The detectives from Dublin Castle descended on the *Evening Press* and wanted to take the negative. We said no: it remained, and would remain, our exclusive property until well after midnight. the *Irish Press* had the right to it exclusively among the morning papers. We were not going to make a present of it to our opposition by having the gardaí distribute it to all and sundry.

The *Daily Express* demanded a copy of the picture, arguing a deal had been done with their man, Bedell. The management replied the only deal was with the photographer who surrendered the negative and all rights for the agreed fee. (Some four years later, Cliff, in a rather rare bout of drinking, burst into the *Irish Press* newsroom one night and denounced me loudly for indulging in "yellow journalism tactics" much to the surprise and amusement of Bill Redmond who noted "that compliment has been coming to you a long time").

117

CHAPTER ELEVEN

We did eventually make copies available to the police who used them in police bulletins and made slides of them to show in cinemas through the country.

The photograph was indeed to be a vital clue in the finding and identifying of baby Pauline Ashmore and again it would be the *Evening Press* who would scoop the pool.

We were a young paper then and fighting hard to establish ourselves. We had a small tight staff and for the first two years we never went to lunch. A pint of milk and a few of Mulligans' sandwiches and that did us. Some of us drank so much milk in those days that we managed to escape the inevitable badge of the hard drinking newspaperman: the stomach ulcer. Jack Smyth of Galway, always trim and trig in his light-blue suit with the waistcoat, manned the desk behind us, two fingers picking out a story like a frantic woodpecker.

When you have a big news-making story like a kidnapping you can be sure that every oddball in creation is going to ring the newspapers. Smyth had briefed us after the first few screwball calls came it.

"Never mind: listen to all of them. Never mind them being screwy: they're reading our paper and that's what we want. Just tag along with them: they're paying customers". So when someone rang and said he was a diviner and could tell us where to find Baby Pauline, we said sure thing, we're listening. Or, yes Mr. So and So: we were very interested. We never cut anyone short.

And then oddest of oddball calls came to Smyth one lunchtime.

The voice said: "I want to report a medical miracle".

Smyth, on red alert, said "Yes?"

"I have just found out about a Dublin woman who gave birth to a child three months ago - and to another last night."

"Yes" said Smyth, "do we have an address for her?"

The caller gave an address. And he was sure she gave birth to another baby? Yes, three months ago.

Smith said "Three months - that's when Pauline Ashmore was kidnapped".

The caller hung up. The line went dead.

Smyth called Jim Flanagan, a former *Roscommon Herald* staffer and said it sounded crazy but we had better check it out. Like all of us, Flanagan had the picture of Pauline etched on his brain, especially the birth mark on her forehead. Flanagan took a taxi to the address and saw the baby then being looked after by her 'grandmother'. He had no doubt as to her identity. He thanked the people in the house and phoned Smyth. Smyth sent a taxi for the Ashmore family and brought them to the home. Mrs. Ashmore looked at the baby and repeated the selfsame phrase: "That's my baby".

Reunited now, Smyth called the Gardaí at Dublin Castle and told the police the news. The Ashmores came to Burgh Quay and the Women's Department looked after them while we had the family photographed from all angles.

Again we were not going to make a present of the Ashmores to the late editions of the opposition papers and while the Fleet Street papers growled about the *Evening Press* "imprisoning" the Ashmores, we waited jubilantly for our final - and very special - city edition.

EVENING PRESS SCOOP LEADS TO THE DISCOVERY OF THIRD MISSING DUBLIN CHILD.

That was the splash headline with mother and daughter pictured, and pictured again with our own Jim Flanagan.

Once more there were police ructions. Again it seemed the *Evening Press* had left the force flat footed. Only this time the opposition - and one other paper had got the same call as Smyth had taken but dismissed it as "another madman on the Ashmore thing" - that suggested that the *Evening Press* got the tip from a police source. The Burgh Quay newspapers insisted repeatedly it was not so but someone had to be made a scapegoat and most of us believed then, and still do, that the man singled out was treated most unfairly. As we argued then, there wasn't a policeman or detective in Dublin, given half a chance to solve the Ashmore kidnapping, who wouldn't have elected to cover himself in glory rather than passing the tip to a newsman who was a complete stranger to him.

Today kidnapping and murder are commonplace happenings: in the Sixties two unsolved kidnappings dominated the news for weeks on end. The Flanagan coup made the *Evening Press* the talk of the city and established its reputation for enterprise and verve.

There was still no news however of the Browne baby, kidnapped over four years previously. The police hunt was renewed for the little girl but it drew a blank. Then, incredibly, a third Dublin child was kidnapped. The Berrigan Baby was snatched from a pram and disappeared as mysteriously as the others. The father was a C.I.É. worker and the family lived in Moss Street, near City Quay.

Once again The Kidnap Team in the *Evening Press* - all Westerners (Jim Flanagan and Jim Downey from Leitrim and Mick Finlan and myself from Mayo), made the twice a day trek to the Berrigans. It is never a pleasant sight to see a mother cry and we tried to make up for invading the family's privacy by trying to reassure them the baby would be found. Look at the Ashmores, we said. The Fleet Street gang were, as always, out and well armed with cheque books. We hadn't cheque books but we did have time to be human beings. Others might knock on the door and politely ask if there were any developments and be glad to be off when the woman shook her head but we did genuinely try to keep their spirits up. To a degree there was a sort of trust in the *Evening Press* men.

It was Christmas week and we kept on saying with God's

help they'd be all together for Christmas but we were not really at all sure.

This time the story broke in Belfast. One or two witnesses had come forward to say they had seen a woman with a baby on the Belfast train from Dublin on the evening of the Berrigan baby's disappearance. The Royal Ulster Constabulary investigated the reports. Late in the afternoon came a report that a woman had been held for questioning. Now the race was on to get to the Berrigans little flat in Moss Street. The *Evening Press* team, now doubling up as the *Irish Press* team, made it in a neck and neck finish with the man from the *Daily Telegraph*, the inimitable George Burrows who was their man in Dublin. George, not being a staffer, hadn't a cheque book to brandish, and when the tug-o-war started, the friendship built up with the Berrigans was enough for Mrs. Berrigan to announce: "We're with *The Evening Press*". Mick Finlan had a taxi waiting and rushed the parents into it as other taxis drove up. Burrows refused to surrender: Mick says he ran alongside the taxi pointing out he was first on the scene.

After the short journey to Burgh Quay the Berrigans were rushed into the security of the building where they had a meal and time to adjust before making the journey to Belfast.

Again the opposition camped outside Burgh Quay in the hope of a snatch picture of the couple. But a taxi drew up at the works entrance. Benedict Kiely and Mick Finlan held the doors open while the parents rushed into their seats, the reporters and photographer with them. The dash to Belfast was on.

When there was a big story on you didn't go home. Under Jim McGuinness, the Derry born editor of the *Irish Press*, the paper went for bright, breezy, tightly written stories, more reminiscent of Fleet Street's *Daily Express* than the old *Irish Press*. Under the old regime when a story broke that had

121

a two or three city dimension to it, each man would write and file copy separately and the sub-editors would rewrite them into a common story. McGuinness favoured the American newsroom usage of the rewrite man being a reporter and more and more I found myself with the task of writing the splash or lead story.

That night there were maybe three or four stories between Dublin and Belfast running between the Belfast staff and Finlan and Kiely.

The woman charged with taking the Berrigan baby was married and living on a neat housing estate in the suburbs of Belfast. She had a sixteen year old son and she had a daughter of four and a half years.

When I wrote the sentence it hit me like a thunderclap. There's too big a gap between the son and daughter of four and a half - and wasn't the Browne Baby just six months old when she was taken four years ago?

I turned to Bill Redmond behind me on the news desk. I told him the hunch I had: wasn't it worth checking out - maybe she has the Browne baby?

"Mister Healy" said Bill, "one kidnapped baby will do us for tonight, thank you. Now move the story up, like a good man."

It kept niggling me but Redmond was right: one kidnap at a time was enough and we had the inside track having 'custody' of the Berrigans.

The story was finished by eleven that night and we had a lull and I went back to Bill. He agreed the gap could be significant and added:

"You can be sure the police will check that, don't worry".

Our team covered itself with glory that night, beating the opposition hollow. There was a descent to the Abbey Street headquarters of Independent Newspapers by Mr T.V. Murphy himself and those who were there said it was like God gifting

Moses with the tablets of stone, except on this occasion, the commandment had been reduced to one: the staff had better wake up and show some of the enterprise of Burgh Quay or get out.

It worked. Their Belfast Office, obviously finding the gap between the charged woman's two children hard to explain, started to make inquiries from the woman's husband about the birth of the four and a half years old girl. A good old fashioned bit of slog work by the *Independent* lads failed to elicit a record of the birth or a baptismal certificate and the *Evening Herald* broke the story that the young girl's identity was being investigated and she could be the Browne baby.

This time we were scooped by the *Independent*. Jim Kelly's team in Belfast had scored. The R.U.C. moved in and the Browns were brought to Belfast by the Gardaí to identify the girl.

It was Christmas week.

Bill Redmond sent me to Belfast on Christmas Eve when the story was, to all intents and purposes, dead. The woman was charged with one kidnapping and it was most likely a second charge would follow. In strict point of law, the case was now *sub judice*.

I went to the house where Bernadette Browne had lived for four years, surrounded by love and care of a kind her parents in Dublin perhaps could not have given her because their circumstances were vastly different. On the chimney breast was a mirror with the legend 'Merry Christmas to all". Beside a smouldering fire, the woman's husband, Ernie, sat alone. He was a broken man. I offered him my sympathy and we sat in silence. Then the whole and tragic story came gushing from him.

He had met his wife in a cinema and she had a son: they married. He had wanted a child of his own and his wife had become pregnant a number of times but always lost the children in a series of miscarriages. She had not got an easy time from some of the neighbours. They used to taunt her for not being able to "hold a child".

One time she became pregnant again and this time things seemed to go well. She had gone away and when she returned she had this baby girl with her. It was Bernadette. A fine big child and feeding well.

Was he suspicious?

Not at all - man alive he was so happy to have a child of his own! He was working for the Corporation and he looked for overtime, every minute he could get, so as to have nice dresses for the wee girl.

Ernie was happy then but he'd be happier having a son like, and he told his woman that. She told him again she was expecting and he was naturally delighted. She'd go away and tell him it was for the doctor and he passed no heed and then she came home with this fine baby boy and it was the greatest thing that could happen them all at Christmas. He hung up the decorations and put Happy Christmas on the mirror and he had all them toys you see over there for Bernadette and the wee boy...

It took all my time to focus my eyes on the pile of toys lying packed on the couch, for you would have to be a stone not to be affected by his story. In forty-eight hours his whole world had crumpled. He didn't mind the loss of the wee boy - but to lose Bernadette after all these years...

The man was an innocent. Even now any suspicions he might have expressed when his wife explained things, he accepted because he knew no better. Now he had lost everything and everyone.

I had lived with the other side of the story for the same four years because for the first six months of the Browne kidnapping it was down to Corporation Place every morning to check if there were any developments. There was little to report and finally it petered out of the news.

Once you've watched mothers sob uncontrollably you want to denounce the fiends who cause so much suffering. Yet now, in the home of a double-kidnapper, a double fiend, you have nothing but sympathy for a poor unfortunate human being who was driven by the social pressure of bad-mouthing neighbours and the ambitions of a very loving and simple husband to risk a second kidnapping which failed.

To tell the other side of the story was as distressing as reporting the experiences of the Ashmore and Berrigan parents. The woman wasn't a fiend. Indeed we came, very quickly, to realise a behavioural pattern which is quite common in baby-snatching cases.

The public had been left with the implied picture of a vindictive kidnapper who had to be something of a monster for trying to do it twice. I wanted to offer the other side of the picture and the trust which a husband had put in his wife.

I sat down and wrote the story on Christmas Day. The *Sunday Press* would be the next publication. I called Editor Matt Feehan and told him what I had, saying I thought it would be *sub judice* but we were outside the jurisdiction and would he run it?

"My good man, John, of course I'll run it - but you go back and have Ernie sign each page giving us permission to use it."

I went back. The therapy of having got his story across made him less upset. He read the story and initialled each page.

I came home to my own wife and family and celebrated a Christmas belatedly. It wasn't for the first time and it wasn't the last.

That's newspapering!

John Healy at work in the newsroom of the *Holyoke Transcript-Telegram*, Massachusetts, U.S.A.

Douglas Gageby - Editor, *Evening Press*.

TWELVE

My years in the *Irish Press* Group were good years. True there had been no willingness to help me to get to America in 1957 to work for the *Holyoke Transcript-Telegram*, in a four month U.S. State Department Exchange programme. A trip I might not have made but for the generosity of my schoolfriend, neighbour and colleague, Ted Nealon who gave me the price of a one-way ticket to New York.

America was great if you were an American. But I was - and this was my great discovery - an Irishman, with a very old country if a young nation state. And Ireland would be my country and since I would live here and bring up my family here, I would insist on doing everything I could to shape it and make it a better country.

It sounds pompous even now, but so fierce was the new passion - as intense as was the initial desire to shake the dust of Ireland forever from my shoes - that I never considered it pompous. I lacked a lot of things but I had one talent: I had, though I realised it only dimly, a whole new value system. I had been at the coalface, and seen that part of the America I had practically worshipped.

Part of that worship had been the devouring of American news magazines and when *Time* or *Newsweek* or *Saturday Evening Post* came up with a new word like "snafu" it never went too many weeks before I had it in print in a story. Like so many words which enjoy a short life it has disappeared: it meant cock-up, simply, a bad mistake.

I was going to write from America, of course. If Alistair Cooke could do it, so could Healy.

A week went by and I wrote nothing. I wanted to get the feel of the place. Two weeks and nothing. The first month and the only thing I wrote was a weekly letter to the family.

It was not until I returned home that I sat down and wrote five pieces. They could be called "reflective". I sent two of them to Des Fisher, London editor of the *Irish Press*, who telexed me from there to say that if the remaining three pieces were as good, the American experience had matured me enormously.

* * * * * * * * *

AMERICA - THE LAND OF EXTREMITIES

They say some people live all their lives in America and never grasp the full and complete picture of the American scene. After five months of watching, listening and studying intensively, an Irishman begins to understand why. For here is a vast country of many extremes; extremes of weather, habits, virtues, vices, ways of living and religion. It is a country where the generosity of the man-in-the-street has contributed billions of dollars so that Europe can sleep safe at night and Asians and Africans eat better - and where a man's life will be taken for a ten dollar bill.

It is at once the most unselfish country in the world, where some of the most selfish men in the world live; it is, too, the most democratic country in the world where the most undemocratic things can, and do, happen. It is a land of opportunity where men and women can in one hour make a fortune and where some people work all their lives to keep ahead of the debt-collector. Most of all, it can be a bewildering country where you find yourself groping for adjectives to describe something and find yourself impoverished because of the staggering immensity of the institutions and the projects they engage in - especially when you come to try and interpret them in terms of Ireland. The way of living is at once the best in the world and the worst in the world (the interpretation of 'worst' depending on the tastes of the observer). And, for all of that, it is a great country. Its greatness probably lies in the fact that it can take all those conflicting extremes and weave them into the unit that is today America, the leading power in the western world and the hope of western civilisation in a third world war.

It's easy for an Irishman to be proud in America for here the Irish have contributed - probably more than any other race - in relation to the size of the mother country - to the growth and expansion of the United States. A century ago they were the poor immigrants, grubbing in the steel mills and furnaces, an education starved people who got only the donkey work and whose brute strength and capacity for hard work were exploited to dig canals and send railroads snaking out across this vast continent from the cities of the east.

Today their grandsons and granddaughters - with the benefit of an education which a free America gave them - occupy the top posts in the land. They lead industry, commerce and are still pioneers. But now, instead of the covered wagon and the shotgun, they use the scalpel, the atom and nuclear power to find new frontiers of knowledge. They fight disease, ideologies and stand guard over a great nation. You'll find them in the key posts of Universities, in research laboratories and in the Government administration centres in Washington. If, and when, a green light flashes a historic "go" which will send the globe-straddling B-52's winging their way into the heart of Russia with a cruel cargo of hydrogen death, one of the men will be Aircraft Commander Major P.J.

Sullivan, who - at this moment - knows the exact details of every street of that Russian town as well as his father knew the streets of Dingle fifty years ago. For you'll find hundreds of Irishmen in the elite of the American armed forces - S.A.C. the Strategic Air Command.

The old maxim, "There's an Irishman in there somewhere" holds equally good in the other not-so-proud world: the world of crime. For just like any other race, they've had - and today still have - their black sheep. In the Senate Rackets Investigation Committee hearing which I attended in Washington the two men who did most of the squirming had Irish names. But in the recent, highly publicised Dave Beck scandal there's an Irishman on the right side of the law. Today most of the Washington commentators credit sixty-seven-years-old John Francis English, a tight-lipped son of a Connaught man with being the man who could have saved Beck from the inevitable plunge from the summit as Chief Executive of the giant Teamsters' Union to ignominious obscurity. John English's biggest no - and his most impressive one - came when Beck told the world that his Union was going to spend one million dollars on a publicity campaign from coast-to-coast to tell the American public "my side of the story," this after he had hidden behind the Fifth Amendment and refused to answer questions as to whether or not he had used Union funds for his own use. English said: "We will not pay one million dollars for any campaign. No campaign for Mr. Beck is planned or under consideration."

So Dave Beck was publicly stripped of what prestige he had after his refusal to testify. And English helped to wipe out the bad taste left in the mouths of the American public by the other lower-echelon Irishman involved on the wrong side of the fence.

It would be wrong to judge the Irish in America by the headline-makers, for there are millions of Irishmen and women who live lives out of the spotlight of television, radio and newspapers. Most of them are proud of their mother country, retain their national language and traditional ballads and dances. They are priests and doctors and plumbers and pawnbrokers, engineers and jet-age aces. They come from Kerry, Mayo, Cork and Galway, Cavan and Clare - from all over the country - to mingle and mix, work and play and join American to make up and become the part of Main Street, U.S.A.

WHITE, BLACK OR JUST AMERICANS

Earl Williams has never met Earl Warren though it's quite likely that Earl Warren has heard Earl Williams. Most certainly, the Chief Justice of the United States is in sympathy with Earl Williams. For Earl Williams, a man honoured by one of the greatest countries in the world, is a man who must be careful where he sits and who he sits with. More exactly still, he must be careful of the colour of the skin of the people among whom he sits.

Earl Williams is much more than a negro; he is one of the greatest, if not the greatest, single problem facing a democratic United States of America. I met Earl Williams in Bourbon Street, New Orleans, where he sings and leads one of the few jazz bands in the French quarter, where jazz was born and grew up. An extremely intelligent men, Williams was well aware of all the absurd paradoxes of segregation.

"Very shortly," he said in his quiet, matter-of-fact voice that had a lot of patience and understanding in it, "I will broadcast to the world. I have made three recordings for 'The Voice of America,' which you will hear in Europe. Yet, here in my own city I must ride at the rear of the bus and must use toilet facilities marked "Coloured only". You and I can ride in a hotel elevator together, yet when we get ten yards away to ride a bus we must separate. Oh, yes, the bus seats are the same; there is no material difference in the actual seats. In fact, if you watch when there are a large number of negroes, you'll see the conductor shift the little bar which says "Coloured only" up a few seats so as to make more room for the negro passengers".

"The white people go to baseball games and cheer their heads off when a negro ball player makes a good play - yet they herd us into one section of the ballpark as inferiors. But it will end - it's all so absurd that it must end. It has started with the Supreme Court and the changes brought about in the short time since are most encouraging. Time and good government will end this curse. . . we have to be patient and fight our battle quietly and legally. We are doing this. . ."

It is hard for us in Ireland to understand why a country where democracy is such a jealously guarded commodity - and a country which was embroiled in two wars because of a hatred for dictatorships - tolerates the injustices of segregation. It is hard for us to appreciate the illogical actions of those who deprive a large segment of the population of elementary civil liberties. The negro question is one of civil liberties. And civil liberties is the biggest question in the United States just now. It is not only the negro; it is the Jew, the Pole, the Italian, the Irishman, the Puerto Rican, the Mexican.

That it should centre round the negro, the Puerto Rican or the Jew is due to the fact as Mr Oscar Cohen, National Programme Director of the Anti-Defamation League in New York says, that those three have "a high visibility." In other words, you can see at first glance that a man is a negro, a Puerto Rican or a Jew, and so it is easier to discriminate against them.

The Constitution and the laws of the United States in theory and - for the most part - in practice give every man, irrespective of colour, creed or national origin equal rights and privileges and full equality designed to guard against discrimination. But the wily element have found ways to go along with the law and yet carry on the policy of discrimination.

133

States Oscar Cohen: "There is more anti-Semitism in the U.S. than in any part of the free world. For instance, our League made a survey of Chicago employment exchanges and found that in thirty per cent of the jobs available no Jews would be accepted. Of the one thousand five hundred travel agents polled, twenty-three per cent of the resort hotels would not admit Jews".

In the case of the negro - a much more publicised one - straightforward: they just ignore the Supreme Court rulings. This autumn, for instance, more schools are due for desegregation. Yet in Maryland State, within the shadow of Washington and Congress, public leaders proclaim that they will shut down all State schools rather than allow negro children to sit with whites. (They have threatened to build private segregated schools to maintain the *status quo*.) In the case of property, land owners discriminate against negroes and Jews by embodying clauses in contracts that the dweller will not do anything to "change the character of the neighbourhood".

With immigrants - as always - came the feeling of fear that hungry mouths would mean (as it often did) cheap labour. Cheap labour meant worsening conditions for the 'natives'. So the Jewish immigrant was discriminated against, as were the Irish and the Italian and the Slavs and German and Dutch. But the Jew was quick and resourceful and was the first to organise and fight back. Because he was barred from many of the professions like engineering and medicine - and because he was never allowed to hold executive jobs - he went into business for himself. (In fact, he was forced into it.)

So today the Jews control much of the business wealth of America, something which continues to propagate the legend of the money-grabbing Jew and helps to make them more hated still. He has prospered fantastically because there were no restrictions put on him by his own private enterprise. And so today in Florida where, in 1880 the first Jews were refused admission to the hotel resorts, they own the billion-dollar strip they call Miami Beach.

It must also be recorded that some Jewish concerns discriminate now, too. There are hotels which do not welcome the "Gentiles" and it is done by simple expedient of making it uneconomical for guests to stay by charging exorbitant rates. But the Jew has one big advantage in the matter of civil liberties which the negro in the South doesn't have: he can exercise his vote and thereby have some say in the election of public officials who will legislate for him. In the "deep South" of the U.S., where the negro technically has a right to vote, the men who a century ago would be the white masters are still the white masters, with this difference: instead of physical slavery they do it by making it impossible for him to vote.

Explained Cohen: "There is a test for applicants - they must identify phrases of the Constitution. You would want to be a sixty-four thousand dollar man to answer some of the qualifying questions. Then there are no facilities in some places for registration. No furniture provided in the booths. And, of course, the fear of physical violence if they do vote."

Will it end as Earl Williams forecast? Oscar Cohen, who was one of the panel taking part in the State Department sponsored seminar which I attended in Easton, Pennsylvania, predicts: "It will. In the last ten years there has been a revolution - a quiet one - in the thinking on the negro question. It has made fantastic progress. School desegregation is going very well, and the next thing to tackle is the right to vote. But it will be a struggle."

But the walls are crumbling. In the North already the negro has equality and enjoys practically all the facilities of the white neighbour. What discrimination exists is of the hidden kind - in the buying of property.

CHAPTER TWELVE

IS THE U.S.A. THE IRISH UTOPIA?

Ireland can be proud of the Irish in America. Ireland can also be sad. Ireland can be proud and sad because so many Irishmen have proven themselves and, in competition with the brains and brawn of other European national races, the Irishman has come out on top in what is the most competitive country in the world: the United States of America.

Today the Irish in America are a respected entity; they have achieved a position in the melting-pot where other emigrant races look up and say "I wish I were an Irishman". It has not always been so and there are still places where the Irishman is called "an ignorant Mick" with the same sneering tone that some of our own less tolerant Irish in America use when they talk of "the ignorant Polacks" or the "dirty wops".

But in the last fifty years, the Irish have raised their sights higher than the lowly but pensionable jobs with City Hall to branch into the fields of business, industry, art, the professions and labour relations field. Because today our educated emigrants are welcomed by employers in any field you want to name, it is something of a mystery to us at home why men and women who were regarded here as "pretty average" do well when they go to America.

Do they do that well? Is America Utopia for the Irish man or Irish girl? America has one great advantage, though it is less present today than it was fifty years ago: opportunity. There is the opportunity to work, and there is recognition for work done whether by promotion, increased salaries or both. And the quick-thinking man can still make a fortune in America.

It's not thirty years ago since a young red-headed youth from Rossmore, Tipperary, was asked to pay a fee while he served his time in a Dublin pub. Timmy Ryan didn't see why he should have to pay to be allowed the privilege of filling stout into bottles. He emigrated. He worked by day, studied by night, got himself a Government job in the Federal Income Tax Bureau. Two years ago, Tim Ryan - he's still the right side of forty - had a discussion with some Irish nuns one night in Houston, Texas. They remarked that it was extraordinary that with all the Irish hospitals - or hospitals run by Irish sisters - in Texas and the adjoining States, there was nobody Irish in the distribution end of the hospital supplies and equipment. That was enough for me", Ryan told me over a dinner in Houston.

He promptly resigned from the Bureau, established credit for ten thousand dollars in the bank, sought and got the concession to distribute a variety of lines from operating tables to bandages and has not looked back since. I examined his books at his request; I saw preparations he was making to open two new offices in St. Louis and Louisiana. By all the standards you want to apply, Tim Ryan is a big success. Tim is happily married, has all the money he wants. There is only one thing wrong: Tim Ryan is sorry that he could not run his business in Ireland and for Ireland but the opportunities aren't there. "I go home to see my mother fairly regularly - she's Mrs. Johanna Ryan of Rossmore in Tipperary - and I find it hard to believe that there are still shopkeepers and publicans who advertise for 'strong farmer's son to train as counterhand, no fee required". This thing of two pounds a week to a young boy and girl behind a counter is nonsense. I mean, I cannot blame them if they grab at the opportunity to emigrate to a country where their initiative, native charm and naturally friendly manner will bring them not only better salaries but quick promotion," argued Ryan.

It's often been said that the Irish in America have a vast amount of goodwill for Ireland. That's very true. And the day that we organise that and use it, will be the day that our economic picture will change. Never mind the stories about the Irish never being able to stick together; the generosity of the Irish in America is something you must watch and

137

experience to appreciate.

I saw, in Brooklyn, a group of Irishmen get together and in one fortnight organise a benefit which drew in six thousand dollars for a colleague who was down on his luck, jobless and in hospital. Many an Irish parish church has been built on American dollars. And long before the American Congress ever sanctioned Foreign Aid in the late 1940's, the Irish were administering the most ideal foreign aid programme of all - on a ten cent stamp! (It was ideal because it was done in the privacy of the mail and with thousands of twenty-five and fifty dollar cheques twice or three times a year to families and relatives - often unseen and unknown - in Ireland.)

Let us not only remember that but remember also that those same givers had to work hard, and still have to work hard, to earn the money for these cheques. Nobody picks money off the streets in America; there is no likelihood that they will ever pick money off the streets either.

Are they, then, happy in America? Materially, yes. But I have no doubt that if they had the same opportunity in Ireland they would return home and gladly work here. They would trade the cocktail cabinet for the opportunity to bring up their family in Ireland; they miss the football and hurling matches, they miss the temperate climate, they miss - and this is very important - the Catholic atmosphere; the leisurely way of life; everything, in fact, that makes Ireland, as viewed from America, seem a magic land when compared with the physical presence of America and the American way of life.

Sometimes they arrive back to find their dreamings and the realities of twenty or thirty years later don't match and there is disappointment. They return after their glorious Mayfly-like appearance and are dead to Ireland. There are other types, of course, but they are in the minority. There is the despicable "professional" Irishman who flourishes exceedingly well in New York. He is slick loud-mouthed and has "all the right connections". There is the other minority who left Ireland during British rule who still think that O'Connell Street, Dublin, is patrolled by British forces! And there is finally the small minority which never got beyond the menial job, never rose above the poolroom and the can of beer simply because they lacked ambition.

Those minorities might make you mad you think. They don't. You pity them. But I'll tell you what does made you mad - what maddened me more than all the loud-mouthed, shamrock-and-shillelagh-waving thugs. It's this: to see so many of our fine men and women, boys and girls, out there doing everything we so desperately need them to do at home; working hard, marrying early, producing families of six, eight and ten children, setting up on their own and employing more Irishmen and women. You'll see them in New York, Boston, Chicago, San Francisco, Detroit, Texas, Philadelphia, Baltimore, Washington - name any State in the Union and any city in that State and you'll find - as I found - successful Irishmen. My own schoolmates are among them - they've started families; families which are lost to Ireland.

You also begin to wonder - and know the answer in your heart and soul before you ask the question - if Irish employers and Irish business concerns place a little too much reliance on hoary experience and not enough on youthful initiative. In America they've made a god of the youthful executive and are breeding, as a consequence, a generation of executives, some of whom are unsure of themselves simply because they "came up too fast". There's a happy medium.

Hidebound Irish managements may frown at the idea of placing a twenty-eight-years-old man on a board of directors or making him factory supervisor. They may say: we gave them their chance and they didn't do anything wonderful. Most of the men I met claimed they didn't get the chance; claimed, too, that unless they were "over sixty" there would be no point in trying to argue for the introduction of new methods or of 'getting on'. Said one Kerryman: "If you try talking a new idea with the boss in Ireland and you're under forty, you'll be told it's not so long ago since you learned to wipe your nose for yourself. That attitude isn't helping Ireland." "Tell them at home," said one twenty-nine-year-old Kerryman "that all we've learned since we came out here, is how to live properly. But most of all, be sure to tell them we didn't pick up any brains or any extra facility for hard work just by crossing the Atlantic. There are a lot of people in Ireland who think the Americans issue us with backbones and brains the minute we step on Pier Eighty-Six in New York. They don't. We grew them at home and brought them with us."

And that's Ireland's pity. . .

THE MIRACLE ROADS OF THE U.S.A.

One of the things which fascinate Irish people about America is the traffic of its cities and roadways. And those who get a quick glimpse at New York and maybe travel down towards the Connecticut Valley on the Merrit Parkway come away with the smug feeling that they can now understand why, in one long national holiday week-end Americans can kill something like four hundred people on the public road.

Some come back to Ireland and publicly thank God that Ireland doesn't have those "racetracks" and "highway race-courses". It is all very stupid. For one of the greatest feat of American engineering - which is really a science with many fine feats to its credit - is the system of roadways which it has built in the East and Midwest of America.

Like many other things, the American Turnpike, parkway, highway, thru-way (they are basically nothing more but different names for the one thing) is an American institution. From New York they go snaking out across the face of this vast country; mile upon mile of long straight and seemingly unending road, more often than not full of sixty miles-an-hour traffic - cars, trucks, truck-and-trailer and buses - moving like regular conveyor belts in two lines one going east, the other going west.

I witnessed the opening - and was one of the first passengers to ride on - America's later super road: the Massachusetts Turnpike, which runs from Boston to the New York State line. It is typical of the three thousand (almost) miles of turnpikes. It not only helps you to get beween two points in a quicker time: it also allows you to do it more safely, but with less wear-and-tear on your vehicle.

Consider it. The journey from Holyoke to Boston was something over ninety miles. Before the turnpike was opened it took something like two-and-half hours of fast and unsafe, because much of the route was two-way undivided traffic, and was exposed to all the hazards that an Irish highway is exposed to: sudden appearances of other traffic, children - all the things which go to make up accident statistics. In addition you had to brake coming into corners, accelerate and change gears on hills - all of which went to make for more wear and tear on your car.

Then came the turn-pike. You drove for a mile or so outside Holyoke, found the entrance to the turnpike, drove up to the barrier, got a ticket on which was punched the time and the gate number you entered the turnpike. You went through the barrier and on to the turnpike, went into top-gear - and drove for eighty-seven minutes without doing a thing other than holding the car on the road!

No gears. No braking. No de-clutching - nothing.

You don't have to sit on edge watching for a youngster or a cow straying on to the road in front of you. They couldn't. For the turnpike is raised up; a platform-like ribbon - like some giant runway on an aircraft carrier, isolated on both sides and therefore free of interruptions (other than those widely-spaced official entrances and exits). And, of course, traffic is one-way and your half is capable of holding four lanes of traffic. And after eighty-seven minutes you leave at the other end. At the exit barrier, you surrender your ticket. The time is checked to see if you exceeded the sixty-miles-an-hour speed limit (I got a raised eyebrow and an "It's-OK-this-time" for clocking ninety miles in eighty-seven minutes!) and you pay something like one and a half pence a mile for the ninety miles.

Of course you have to pay. But it pays you to pay. It pays the big manufacturing firm to send their trucks on the turnpikes even when they must pay nearly twenty five shillings for a two hundred and forty mile journey. Why? Because the efficiency experts and engineers have proven that they will get a longer and more trouble-free life out of their trucks. And get their goods there faster - which cuts down overtime bills for truckers as well as allowing them to promise earlier delivery.

But most important of all is this factor: if America did not have a system of dual highways, its statistics of road deaths, now at forty thousand a year, would be nearer the one hundred thousand mark. Subtract three thousand miles of one-way roads, replace them with traffic travelling in both directions on the same roads and see what happens. We know what happens in Ireland. We know it from the records of what happened on the Bray Road *before* and *after* one stretch of it was split down the middle to divide the traffic. The incidence of fatal accidents fell sharply (You can have accidents on a turnpike, but they are the result of speed wobbles; eliminate the danger of head-on collisions and you reduce the number of fatal accidents).

There have been many pious resolution passed by many bodies in Ireland for the past couple of years in an effort to reduce Irish road fatalities. There have been some people who campaigned for greater safety on the roads, yet at the same time in the same breath - attacked the building of bigger and wider roads as folly and unnecessary expenditure. They said such roads would be "speedways for drunken drivers". In most instances they quoted the example of the Naas Road which - though one of the widest in the country - has a big fatality rate, as the reason why the nation shouldn't have wider and better roads.

Over a year ago I discussed road safety with the top experts in Ireland and Britain, in a series on the subject for this paper. The American experts did nothing more than reinforce the arguments that road safety is a vital matter for the engineers and that they can, in a large measure, do much to solve it. In the Custom House in Dublin, the engineers employed by the Department of Local Government have already mapped out what might be the Irish equivalent of the turnpike.

Engineers measure the standard of road safety by density of traffic; if for any thirty-two hours of the year four hundred vehicles an hour pass a given point on the road, that road should be converted to a dual carriageway. Apply that to the roads out of Dublin, Cork, Galway, Limerick or Belfast and ask yourself how safe they are. Two American-type highways - one from Belfast through Dublin on to Cork and from Dublin across to Galway - would alter not only the shape of the Irish traffic picture; it would also reduce fatal accidents, shorten the time-distance between the points mentioned, and provide a more economical transport system.

RICH MARKETS WAIT FOR US IN THE U.S.A.

Your hard-headed very wise Irish businessman will laugh when you tell him he's missing a fortune by not going to America for a few months! He'll ridicule the idea that just by walking down the main avenue of any American city and watching the windows or department stores, you can pick up two or three small industries. Try and argue with him and he'll tell you: "Oh, the Americans can make that sort of an idea pay - they've got the big population. They've a consumers' market."

I've said a thousand times when asked about America and I'll repeat it again: if I had my way I would insist on sending to America for six months one man from each business concern in this country. I don't care what the "line" or industry is - whether it is selling peanuts or thoroughbred horses - the Irishmen can learn something from their American counterparts.

Americans claim they are twenty or thirty years ahead of us "technologically speaking" (as they say). And they are. And for one reason only: research. I have listened to people at home here getting up and decrying the lack of research facilities here in Ireland. They bemoan the fact that research is "too costly" and consequently they must suffer and go without it and the enormous benefits it brings.

But is Irish industry - are Irish firms - so money starved or so penny-pinching that they cannot afford to invest one thousand pounds once every two or three years to send one of their executives to the United States on a study tour? Or are they really serious when they talk about lack of research facilities in Ireland? For if they are, they can solve them for as little as that - one thousand pounds. For it's been my experience that the American businessman, industrialist, small-town manufacturer, garage proprietor - any line you wish to name - is very eager to throw his house open to a visiting man from abroad. He is desperately keen to know how we tackle our problems. In other words he is eager to exchange ideas and methods.

Is it important to do it? The answer is another question: Are we not now living in an "Export-or-Die" era? Are we not for ever talking of the importance of a dollar market? Can we then survive in the most competitive market in the world if we don't know what the home-based market in America is like, what it is doing, what are its tastes.

Most people would laugh at me - or anyone else - if I said six months ago that oatmeal was a dollar-winner. I'd have laughed myself. But I've

watched Americans rush to the stores for Irish oatmeal! A delicacy! We've
laughed at this thing of leprechauns for American tourists. We've
hesitated to exploit the market. The Japanese didn't. Now we cry when
the Japanese flood the Irish and indeed the American market with badly
made and crudely-shaped leprechauns.

By all means avail of Coras Trachtála and its services. But if you go
out to study and see what the other man is doing, you'll also find your
own markets. They are there. I'm certain of it. And if the hard-headed
over cautious businessmen of this country don't believe it, let them look
at the men who have gone out. We can provide all the incentives we like
to stimulate exports, but if tight-fisted Irish managements are unwilling
to invest three thousand dollars to send a man - or go themselves - to
America, not only to explore the market but to pick up new ideas in
allied fields, and adapt them - or their own ideas - for both the Irish
market and the American market, their own incentives are wasted. And
if the Americans want cakes with green icing on them, give them to
them.

Our competitors don't cavil about colour schemes. If they want light
tweeds, give them light tweeds. Witness the success of the Thurles
shoe-making factory. These men went out to America, brought back
American patents and American machinery and built shoes specifically to
American tastes and patterns. The first week these shoes went on display
in Boston in Jordan Marsh and Filene's, two of the biggest houses in
Boston, managed again by shrewd men and women who throw sentiment
out the window and operate on strictly business lines, they proved a sell
out. (Be it said that C.T.T. were behind this venture.) Is there a need to
spell out the moral?

One can't help being amazed at how well this country does in spite of
the lack of information under which we work. Take our hotels for
instance. What we regard as our leading hotels are, in many ways,

fourth grade hotels by American standards. For in a fourth grade American hotel, each room is equipped with a shower and toilet. Americans are frankly amazed at the idea of walking down a corridor to have a bath or go to the toilet.

Again we can compete very favourably on our own resources if we can only utilise them. We know the American is dollar conscious. Why then - when we will come out very favourably - do we hesitate to name the cost of items in dollars and cents and translate in everyday American terms the cheapness of Ireland's amenities? Again we are losing millions of dollars because we hesitate to spend a few thousand in educating - and this is the crux of the whole thing for a trip to America is one of the greatest educations there is - the comparatively small handful of people upon whom our foreign markets and our international trading, whether in tourism or selling shoes, depends.

Examine any field you wish and see how it applies. We're making souvenirs - but do we know that there are hundreds of thousands of 'antique' shops in America which deal exclusively in selling the souvenirs of other countries? Have we tapped this market? How many of our grocers have ever stood in a supermarket? How many of them have ever studied packaging, displaying, marketing of goods? How many of our experts have studied the economics of deep-freeze and frozen foods? How many of our manufacturers of refrigerating equipment have gone to the trouble of finding out the advantages the American housewife finds in her kitchen refrigerator - and why it is standard equipment in even the most menial home? It is not enough to say that refrigerators are luxuries - good health and good hygiene are not luxuries. No more than economic housekeeping is a luxury. Stimulate business and you stimulate production; stimulate that and you stimulate employment. One could go on for months simply because there is so much to learn, because they have advanced with excellent research facilities.

I've never had any ambitions to be anything other than a newspaperman. But many, many times during my stay in America I did wish I were an industrialist or a businessman with some little capital - even as little as one thousand pounds - for no other reason than to prove that it is possible to go to America, take some of their ideas, and adapt them successfully for Irish market conditions on the home market and for the American market.

But then your hard-headed Irish industrialist will tell you that that is the difference: I'm a newspaperman and know nothing about the worries and headaches of industry and business, and if I did, I mightn't be so sure.

I'd like to meet that challenge. But then I'm quite safe in issuing it. If Irish businessmen who pay fairly heavy company taxes can't see their way to expending one thousand pounds in sending one of their keenest men to America to study the market, they're not likely to worry about a newsman who, after all, knows nothing about the worries and headaches of business.

First printed in the *Irish Press* September 1957.

* * * * * * * * *

On my return, the editor, Jim McGuinness had left. The the new man had very little of the enthusiasm of the Derryman. In today's terms Mr. Carty was more laid back. His background, I think, was more on the literary side and what track record he had was in writing magazine pieces - or so I was told on my return. Truth to tell I was not interested enough to find out, for the American trip had wrought - a word I use with respect - a change in me. I will repeat myself, I went to America impatient to shake the dust and frustrating dirt of Ireland off my shoes. In two months I had two good job offers and I wrote and told my wife, "Evelyn, this is for us." After four months I said: "Take it handy - sell nothing." I came home and - again I repeat myself - if I had had to break stones for the crusher on the roadside, I'd have done it rather than live and rear a family in America.

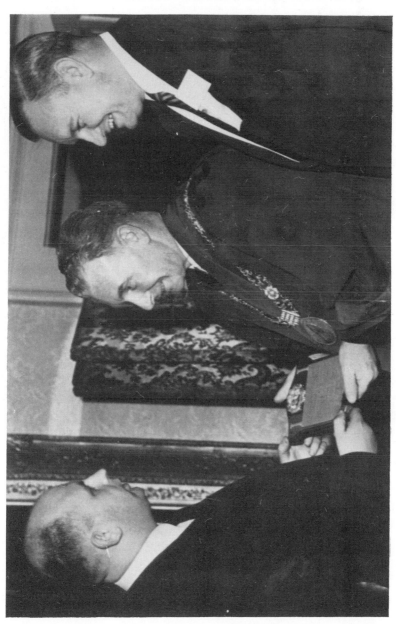

John Healy receiving an award for the St Patrick's Day Parade 1957, Holyoke, Massachusetts U.S.A.

MAR 23 1957

John Healy with members of the 46th Air Rescue squadron as featured in the *Holyoke Telegraph Transcript*.

THIRTEEN

I left the *Irish Press* in the summer of 1959. Douglas Gageby had left the editorship of the *Evening Press* a few months before to go to the *Irish Times* as joint-managing director, a boardroom detail he shared with George Hetherington. Conor O'Brien succeeded Gageby as editor of the *Evening Press*. He inherited a very successful paper. The winning format remained. As far as the reader was concerned, nothing changed: it was as if Gageby never left. For me, however, the rapport which had been established with Gageby over the best part of the Fifties, the excitement of the launch of the *Evening Press*, the battle to make it stick and then go on to become the best selling evening paper, was no longer there.

I was now there long enough to be put through that curious *Irish Press* institution: the loyalty test. It seems an odd system. In the years of Jim McGuinness as editor I was generally rated to be the by-lined, page one reporter, usually involved in the lead story of the day, either as a reporter on the spot or as the rewrite newsroom man who would take copy from maybe half a dozen people and knock it into a coherent lead story.

The system was an American one: the *Irish Press* tended to use the American organisational model where the other houses used the British one. The *Irish Press* had a news editor: in the other houses the same function was filled by the chief

151

reporter. All copy from differing sources would go to the chief sub-editor who would pass it to the 'splash' sub-editor who would edit the contributions into a readable lead story.

After almost a decade working for the group, the question remained: would I be an *Irish Press* 'lifer', in a word, would I give it fealty? The crucible test wasn't really that appalling. After fairly long spells of working ten o'clock to six o'clock and working on the big story of the day, you could find yourself, in high summer, doing the night shift, four in the afternoon to midnight. Mostly you were doubling up as a copy taker. On a muggy July night you were stuck in a booth with a pair of 'cans' on your ears, taking the first, second and third placings at Dysart Agricultural show, not forgetting the reserve category for bulls. And when you had spent thirty sweaty minutes in the booth taking that show you found a local correspondent was on the line with yet another show and another few yards of copy of firsts, seconds and thirds.

There is nothing creative about taking copy. Anyone can do it, given the ability to punch typewriter keys. In fact, we had copy-takers who were far more efficient than the newsroom reporters.

You were getting the doghouse treatment and you knew it as well as the desk knew it. At the end of one long and particularly muggy night when I left the fourth agricultural show on his desk, I said to Bill Redmond, then News Editor, "You know, of course, Margaret Foley (one of the copy takers) can do this far faster than I can. Does anyone in the building ever cost this system or test its efficiency? I am paid a salary for which you could have two girls taking copy: they will take it in half the time I need, so one way or another the firm is losing heavily."

Bill smothered the smile which started at the corner of his mouth and said, "Get that copy up to the chief sub". Then as I turned to do that: "By the way, I've marked you four to twelve for tomorrow." I was sure the smile was no longer smothered but I chose not to look: you don't let them take too much pleasure out of dog-housing.

There were several men older than myself who had been through the system and came out the other side to settle down to a life-long job in the place. Once you broke, once you accepted the bridle, you had a tolerably good life. The Desk knew the kind of assignments you liked and, invariably, you got the pick of the day's press conferences. It might be a country assignment where the expenses would be good, the job not too demanding and the social end of the 'marking' quite acceptable. Life is always a lot more agreeable when you are on drinking terms with the drill-sergeant and Mulligans was a favourite watering hole come six o'clock.

I didn't drink in those days. I was one of the new generation of reporters who wore the "Pioneer" pin. A good many of my generation kept the confirmation pledge not to drink, and if we didn't fit the clichéd role of the hard-drinking, raincoated and slouch-hatted reporters from "Front Page" or all the 'B' movies of the day it never worried us. We could do the job just as well. In the Fifties the *Irish Press* had a particularly good newsroom of reporters, all young men who made their mark in later life, and many more than myself were non-drinkers.

Arthur Noonan went on to become political editor of R.T.É. Ted Nealon became editor of the *Sunday Review* and later went into politics to become Minister for State for the Arts in Garret FitzGerald's second administration. Joe Jennings of Sligo went on to follow Tim Dennehy of Kerry into P.R. in C.I.É. and later became Government Press Officer to both FitzGerald governments. Niall Andrews of Dublin left the Irish Press to become a G.I. in Korea and returned to become a member of the Dáil and, later, a member of the European Parliament. Michael Mills, who remained, became political correspondent of the *Irish Press* and was made the first Ombudsman by the FitzGerald Administration. Maurice O'Brien went on to the P.R. section in the old Hospitals Trust. Michael Finlan went into Canadian broadcasting before returning to Ireland and the *Irish Times*. Jim Flanagan moved to television, just one of the many recruited by R.T.É. Sean Ward went on to succeed Conor O'Brien as editor òf the *Evening Press* while Liam Flynn switched to their art department to become group art editor.

Down the years the *Irish Press* has always had a great newsroom team. As soon as a good story broke, the whole team were in on it. We didn't wait for direction from the news desk and news editor. Every man reached for a phone, one to ring the local garda station, another the parish house, a third some contact he had in the town or village. The Desk had the maturity and good sense to let the team make the initial run to see what it produced. You don't get to sit on The Desk as news editor or assistant news editor unless you've worked the "book" or the full listing in the daily news diary which is the backbone of all newsroom operations. In a working reporter's life in Ireland there will not be too many corners of the country you will not have covered assignments in, and thus have made some contact or other. The good news editor is the person who has built up a contact book or has the gift of total recall so that, when a story breaks, he or she can suggest a starting-point other than the police station.

Jack Smyth of Galway, so tragically drowned at the height of a great career, was news editor of the *Evening Press*. He rarely went to lunch but in that democratic way we had, he'd answer a ringing phone and take a story to get it up to the subs if there was no one else to take it. His replacement, after he drowned in the Liffey, came to Burgh Quay from the commercial side of the house. He took his lunch break not knowing the tradition which had arisen with the evening paper. One day, on his return, he inquired routinely, "Anything happen while I was out?"

I answered off-handedly, "No - everything's quiet".

The last hour had indeed been not merely quiet but positively boring in newsroom terms. However when the news editor had barely left for lunch a call came in, reporting the murder of a young woman. Sean Cryan, who was the crime reporter, was going out the door to his break but doubled back on hearing the word "murder". In double quick time, we had the story wrapped up, and it was on the chief-sub's desk in less than half an hour. Cryan carried on while I held the fort.

The first city edition came up at two-thirty p.m and the news editor read the splash headline:

"WOMAN MURDERED IN DUBLIN:
CITY-WIDE HUNT FOR KILLER"

Very severely I heard him say:

"Mister Healy - I thought you said nothing happened while I was out".

I turned to see him refer to the lead story:

"Oh, that - that happened hours ago, well, just as you went out the door. I thought you meant in the last hour..."

It wasn't the most politic thing to say to a man who knew he was not fitting-in as part of the evening team and especially as Jack Smyth's successor. Yet there was no intention to insult the poor man or 'cut' him in any way. When an hour passes with all its stories in what is a busy newsroom and someone asks you if there's anything happening, the most natural reaction is to say, truthfully, no.

In the Fifties a murder was big, front-page news and might make a lead story for five or six days running. This particular murder, while the lead, was not a great one. It was a husband and wife quarrel which ended with the husband strangling the wife. The formula of "a man was helping gardaí with their inquiries" was as near as you could get to naming anyone pending a formal arrest and charge.

The year was still 1957. The same old men were in Dail Éireann, led by Eamon de Valera. The same old spiteful politics operated. Emigration was rampant but we didn't get mad anymore and shouting "stop" just then seemed to be a fruitless experience.

Dublin wasn't Ireland and I kept reminding myself of that. I had never stopped reading the provincial papers, a habit I developed in the Irish News Agency because the local notes and news were often a first class source. As a reporter in Ballina I was not too long learning that Dublin papers give scant coverage to matters outside "The Pale" and I made the promise, even then, that if ever I got to Dublin I'd do what I could to see "country news" got a fair show.

It was in a local paper, the *Anglo-Celt*, that I first read a squib about a group rearing trout in a burnt out mill on the shores of Lough Sheelin. The group was called The Inland Fisheries Trust and a man called Michael Kennedy was Secretary. I called him. Patiently he explained the objects of the Trust. It had been set up by the Coalition Government under Mr. James Dillon, Minister for Agriculture. Dillon, in power, had embarked on two great projects. The first was The Land Reclamation Scheme, which I had seen in Mayo as the bulldozers moved scrub and heather to make land. Because it was concerned with land it overshadowed his second and complementary scheme, the reclamation of the lakes of Ireland to make them more productive. For every acre of lake water now controlled by pike, he wanted pike and perch-free waters to support a big population of trout. A well managed fishery could produce a ton of trout to so many acres.

The Land Reclamation Scheme was made a political

football. The Inland Fisheries Trust attracted no political flak, for in Ireland we don't think too much about freshwater and its uses, or fish.

Kennedy was a pioneer, a gifted communicator and a civil servant with the gift of creativity and leadership. He literally spent many long hours educating me in the intricate biological work of the Trust to the point where I became something of a specialist in fish culture.

I wrote a series of articles about the team on Sheelin, under biologist Noel Roycroft and ex-Army Sergeant Moss Legatt, and the detective methods used to get a profile of the life and times of the trout, perch and pike on the lake and, from this, a profile of the living lake itself.

Jim McGuinness, himself an angler, was as fascinated as I was and as the readers were to be, to the point where he came back to see if I could continue with another series.

The *Irish Press*, they were so say afterwards, "made" The Inland Fisheries Trust and was to be its sole editorial supporter, a fact which amazed James Dillon himself who regularly and colourfully inveighed against that paper, dubbing it the "Pravda" of Burgh Quay.

In many ways, the first stirrings in the grassroots (one of the Americanisms to which I held on) of what would become The Swinging Sixties, began to appear. The Westport Sea Angling Club held a new sort of festival. For a fortnight anglers from overseas fished Clew Bay and were taking enormous bags each day.

Where had they come from? I got myself detailed to cover the second year of the festival and the answer was astonishingly simple. The Westport hoteliers, instead of sitting on their 'butts' balling out Bórd Fáilte for a bad tourist season, went each winter to France and Germany, and visited U.S. bases, talking about the big fish in Clew Bay, inviting the continentals to visit Westport for a fishing package-holiday.

They came to discover Europe's piscatorial El Dorado, with catches of a lifetime. Irish, European and even world records fell as the Frenchmen especially brought in headline-making catches every day for the two weeks. And every day for two weeks the *Irish Press* had Healy's report on Page One.

I had never fished the sea in my life. Sitting on the shore was one way of covering a festival. Borrowing a rod and getting in amongst the action with fishing machines like Monsieur Fetis or Herr Fuchs, the holder of the world record monkfish at sixty-nine pounds was another way to do it.

The angling magazines of Europe headlined the great bonanza and when it was all over I remember writing a piece on the lines of "How To Start a Fishing Festival and Make a Fortune." Dr. Tim O'Driscoll of Bórd Fáilte loved it and sent a warm private note to say so. A curate in Moville came to see me in Dublin: would I come to Moville and give a talk to a group anxious to run a festival like Westport. Better still, I said, I'd ask the Westport pioneers to do the job. I gave him the names and they gladly travelled to the top of Donegal which, the following year, ran a three-week festival. The pattern was set. Up and down the coast, like a domino effect, sea angling festivals broke out until, by the early Sixties, there was no coastal county in the country which did not have a sea angling festival.

Nor were the stirrings of a new awareness confined to the coastline and the good summer days. In the long winter nights groups were now coming together in what was to become a great national movement and again the West had the headline to set.

The Western Drama Festival in Tubbercurry pre-dated fishing festivals and was rather unique. Once more a handful of people like Joe Masterson, Sean O'Dowd and Dr. Flannery

158

beckoned the committee which, for one week a year during Lent, used the parochial hall for a festival of amateur plays. Matt Devine, Masterson's uncle, had written several one-act plays like "Sugar for Jam" allowing would-be Thespians like Alfie Rochford, later a distinguished District Justice, cut their teeth. Between his works and Lady Gregory's offerings, the winter months were lightened.

On the East Coast, Dundalk had established a drama festival and between these "poles" as it were, the amateur drama movement was born and flourished in the Fifties.

We were also to witness the first stirrings of the greatest movement of all to come out of rural Ireland: the Comhaltas Ceoltóirí Éireann. It was a thirty-two county movement with the Antrim and Derry fiddlers, Presbyterians to a man, playing shoulder to shoulder with men like John Gardner of Ballymote who later settled down to produce a musical family in Dundalk. There was the great Mrs. Crotty of Kilrush whose frail concertina was the catalyst which made the circuit close when she fingered it, releasing jigs and reels and slides and polkas in a new birthing with every playing. She'd talk and argue with you as she played, as if the music was some spring well or reservoir inside her which came welling up, so long as the concertina was on her lap and her fingers on the buttons. There were R.U.C. men who knew the secret joinery of a jig and came to Ennis and Boyle to share it with Michael Gallagher of Donegal, John Doherty, Molly Harrington and Dr. Brian Galligan of Cavan. The men and women who got together every Whit for a week-end of crack and music and singing and dancing in the streets and houses. They carried no cultural campaign banner, they preached no revival gospel and gathered only to play together once in the year.

We called it the Fleadh and the young people, who had turned their back on their own language because it was politicised, soon discovered the exuberant joy of the Fleadh Cheoil. The Clancy Brothers were already big in New York and the rest of America, playing their ballads.

With each Whit the Fleadh grew greater and the Fleadh spirit swept across the face of the nation like a prairie fire. The priests started to worry. Such exuberant enthusiasm for the native music which, having survived in the cabins and bothans on the hills and in some villages, because there were penny whistles, had a new standing. Now the youngsters knew who quiet spoken and easy-going Ciaran MacMathuna was as he went his way on his radio "job of journeywork" and why Seamus Ennis had devoted so much of his life to collecting the old airs as well as playing what he collected.

Looking back now I am sure that we started then to leave behind us the last of the old divisions of the Civil War. The first closing was the way in which the young joined the Army in the 1940's. The sons of Bolshie and Blueshirt families marching shoulder to shoulder on barrack squares from Galway to Athlone from Dublin to Cork, as Harry O'Donovan put it, on the one road, sharing the one load.

In the 1960's the structuralists would move in to "channel" and eventually politicise the Comhaltas on the grounds they had a divine mission to "save the music for the nation". When the troubles in the North broke the politicisers were already in control. How well they knew their own movement was supremely emphasised when in 1970 the annual Fleadh Cheoil was cancelled "as a mark of sympathy for our suffering brethern in the North".

Our suffering brethern were the Northern Catholics and the Nationalist population, the majority of whom never heard of the Fleadh. No mention at all of our Antrim and Derry Presbyterians whose fiddle playing and concert flute players swopped airs with the men from the West and the South and Dublin town in a true republic of music.

The politicisers were too late. The fire had started. The villages and towns and cities were alive once more to the sound of Irish music and Irish airs, and unlike the language, the movement remains vigorous enough to survive the politicisers.

It was a totally changed country from that of the mid-Fifties when Dublin City gave Sean South of Garryowen a massive funeral as his body came through the capital from Monaghan border where he had been killed in an I.R.A. raid on a barrack.

I am sure there are, somewhere in the secret service files, shots of those of us who walked quietly down O'Connell Street and if they had trouble working out who it was flanked Cyril Cusack that day, that was their trouble. We didn't have to think things through that time. It was enough that there was, in our time, a contemporary who cared enough for his country to give his life for it. So you walked and paid the tribute and made your protest against an administration which put the onus on the journalists of the day to make the I.R.A. invisible. Under the Special Powers Act it was forbidden to call the organisation "The Irish Republican Army" or use the designation "I.R.A.". Even when you were quoting an eye witness, we had to change the actual phrase "I.R.A." into "a member of an illegal organisation". Thus if an armed man said: "Hands up - this is the I.R.A." you had to render it: "Hands up - we are members of an illegal organisation".

Section Thirty One was away in the future but the genesis of that restriction did not have to await the arrival of state television.

The new mood towards the end of the Fifties was one in which the people started to rely more on themselves and their own talents instead of waiting for the politicians in Dublin who promised everything and delivered little enough - and that little was generally a right which would come anyway,

CHAPTER THIRTEEN

like the Old Age Pension.

It was good to be on the road then, to encourage this new spirit by the simple means of doing an enthusiastic job of reporting. It was one way those of us who came from rural Ireland could show that there was another country beyond the Pale and it had interesting people doing interesting things which were newsworthy and which, properly reported, made for increased circulation.

In turn I was elected to the National Executives of both the All-Ireland Drama Council and the Irish Federation of Sea Anglers and Comhaltas later proffered the same invitation. By the time that invitation came I had learned very quickly that it is a mistake for a reporter to join any organisation because in a small country like Ireland, sooner or later, there is bound to be controversy and no matter how fair you may be in your reporting or comment, one side - and sometimes both - will regard your comment and reporting partial and partisan. That stage came when the developing amateur drama movement had grown so swiftly that the Athlone Drama Festival, The All-Ireland Drama Festival to give it its full title, found it difficult to cater for the growing number of festivals which had the right to nominate groups to the All-Ireland. There was a lot of controversy over splitting the festival into an urban and rural affair, with the rural All-Ireland transferred to Loughrea, while Athlone retained the prestigious urban-group Festival. As someone who had worked hard to "build-up" the Athlone All-Ireland as one of the events of they year, I had no stomach for seeing rural groups, among them that of my own home-town Charlestown under producer Paddy Henry, denied access to compete for the main trophy and side-tracked into Loughrea. Today it doesn't seem much of an issue. Drama Festivals must now compete for space against daily shootings, killings and bombings. For two decades now the condemning indian prayer wheels are rolled every morning as the latest sectarian killing is recorded. Ireland has become that unique geographical misshapen object, a two-sided nation called the North and the South, with no East or West.

By the summer of 1959 I felt it was getting time to move on. I tendered my resignation to the news desk. Bill Redmond was surprised and disappointed. When he informed the *Irish Press* executives, Major Vivion de Valera asked him to accompany me to his office. The Major was going to sort things out.

The real, deep down, basic reason, I suppose, was that the departure of Gageby for whom I had worked as a reporter, doing the job in my own time, meant a change of regime. I had been used to working independently of "the book" (or news desk) and mightn't show in the office for a few days on end. I would, each night, or early morning, leave in a bundle of copy for the early sub-editor, enabling the early pages to get away.

The copy was not of great importance. I was once again the "paragraphist" turning out what my friends considered to be 'shit copy', a three line paragraph saying that such a person had applied to the Planning Department of Dublin Corporation for permission to erect a lean-to shed at the rear of the premises. I'd have a column or two of those sort of notes covering the entire city and county area.

It was out of one such planning notice, seeking permission to erect a petrol pump at Greygates, Stillorgan, that came one of the first big court actions by residents who were alerted by the three liner, took action to stop it and it ended up in the High Court. Every so often, of course, as you ploughed your way through the planning applications you got a lead on the creation of a new factory or the extension of an existing one, which meant jobs and maybe a page lead story.

An extension of the city hall beat was attending meetings of the local residents' association. They were the infant days of A.C.R.A. and N.A.T.O. and the attention which the the *Evening Press* gave to local problems on the new estates helped to make the paper as THE Dublin evening paper, a role which had previously been reserved for the oldest of them all, the *Evening Mail*. The *Evening Herald* followed the press in trying to cover local affairs but it lacked consistency by failing to appoint one staff person to do the job.

Gageby didn't care if he never saw me from one week to the other so long as the copy was on his desk at eight in the morning: that suited me, too. It was the old lobster trick of the I.N.A. days all over again. So that when I came face to face with Major Vivion de Valera after a spell of taking agricultural shows from four to twelve, I was, for the second time in my life, fairly frank and outspoken. I said that those of us who gave absolute loyalty to the house got dog's treatment while a few who had walked out of the place to go freelancing were treated royally and were making far more money.

"Yes", said Vivion, "but what are you going to do for a job, Mr. Healy - you have a family?"

He smiled when he added that bit, as if it meant he had me by the 'short and curlies'.

"I'm going to freelance - I'm setting up a City Hall service covering the Corporation and Dublin County Council and possibly Dun Laoghaire Corporation."

The smile was gone.

"You would keep our group in mind, I hope."

"Major, you have three papers: I will offer copy to all three as I will to the others".

Coming back from our meeting, Bill Redmond, who towered over most of us, looked down at me and said,

"Young man, you said a lot of things today that might

have been said a long time ago."

There was genuine admiration - and satisfaction too - in his voice: he was pleased for the rest of the week.

But the job in the *Irish Press* was really up and I knew it. I rang Douglas Gageby at home. Could I come and talk to him? I did so with some trepidation because although we had worked in the I.N.A. and the *Irish Press* and he had always encouraged me in what I wanted to do, there was always the remark Bill Redmond once made to a reporter friend of mine as he watched an animated conversation between Gageby and myself at the other end of the newsroom: "One day that young man is going to overstep the mark..."

Major Vivion de Valera

John Healy talks to John Frain on Fair Day, Charlestown, Co. Mayo

John Healy the angler.

APPENDIX

THE NEED FOR AN AGENCY

Before the establishment of the Irish News Agency, Ireland had no news-distributing system of her own. News from Ireland reached the outside world, and news of the outside world reached Ireland, almost entirely through the London offices of the international agencies. This system had serious drawbacks: it meant that news of and for Ireland passed through a filter, not indeed of hostility or bias, but of lack of knowledge. for example, an item of Irish news which might be of real interest in New York or Boston could easily be "killed" in London, where its interest might not be apparent. A similar process took place in the reverse direction. From the perspective of London, Ireland was a remote and inconvenient news-province of the United Kingdom; it was natural in this framework that the coverage of Irish news should be sparse and haphazard. A similar situation had led most of the smaller European countries, after the First World War, to establish their own News Agencies. It was inevitable, after Ireland had established her independence, that she should, sooner or later, set up a national Agency. The reasons why it was "later" rather than "sooner" stemmed from the relative lack of development of the country. The national Press was scarcely large or wealthy enough to undertake the necessary heavy initial investment, nor did there exist groups of wealthy and public-minded industrialists, such as those whom King Albert of the Belgians, in like circumstances, had induced to finance the foundation of the *Agence Belga*. Private enterprise, in short, was not yet equipped to undertake the task, and it became necessary for the State to give the scheme its impetus.

ESTABLISHMENT OF THE AGENCY

The Irish News Agency was set up by Act of the Irish Parliament this year. Its initial financing was supplied by means of repayable advances, and it was provided that the Agency should be directed by an autonomous board. There was provision also for an advisory body, to be composed of representatives of the Irish press. The introducer of the measure, Mr Seán MacBride, Minister for External Affairs - himself a former Agency journalist - made it clear that what was being set up was to be a News Agency in the full sense of the word. He stated as follows in answer to a Parliamentary question: "The Irish News Agency is not an organ of propaganda. It is a medium for the distribution, on a commercial basis, of an adequate objective and impartial service of news and features of Irish interest."

The Board of the Agency, since its setting up, has operated in the light of this definition of its functions.

THE FIRST MONTHS OF PROGRESS

The Board, composed of businessmen, journalists and diplomats, has gathered together a staff of experienced journalists, including leading Agency men from Fleet Street. It has appointed correspondents in every town and most major villages throughout Ireland, and also correspondents in a number of European capitals. The great majority of all Irish newspapers both North and South - for the Agency operates throughout the entire island - have agreed to take a service from the Agency at commercial rates. Significant of the general recognition of the Agency's impartiality was the fact that the first newspaper to conclude a contract with it was the old-established and Conservative *Irish Times*. In Britain, every newspaper so far approached has agreed to accept trial services from the Agency, which secured a sensational "scoop" over all British National dailies within a week of opening up in the British market. Altogether a quarter of a million words were sold in the first three months of operation - a creditable record in view of the fact that this was a period of exploration and the opening up of services.

THE AIMS

The Agency's aims are: (a) To distribute throughout the world, wherever commercial markets can be found, news features and photos primarily but by no means exclusively associated with Irish affairs. (b) To bring into Ireland such news and other press services as can be sold to the newspapers and magazines of the country; to build a press communications system and to organise the collection and distribution of news.

In its working to date the Agency has proved that there is a public demand for the attainment of these objects. It means to exert all its efforts towards the satisfaction of that demand.

Issued by the Irish News Agency - 1953.

ALSO BY JOHN HEALY:

NO ONE SHOUTED STOP
NINETEEN ACRES